# Briefing Your Architect

## 2nd edition

**FRANK SALISBURY**

Architectural Press

Architectural Press
An imprint of Butterworth-Heinemann
Linacre House, Jordan Hill, Oxford OX2 8DP
A division of Reed Educational and Professional Publishing Ltd

$\mathcal{R}$  A member of the Reed Elsevier plc group

OXFORD  BOSTON  JOHANNESBURG
MELBOURNE  NEW DELHI  SINGAPORE

First published as *Architect's Handbook for Client Briefing* 1990
Second edition 1998

**British Library Cataloguing in Publication Data**
A catalogue record for this book is available from the British Library

**Library of Congress Cataloguing in Publication Data**
A catalogue record for this book is available from the Library of Congress

ISBN 0 7506 3642 4

Typeset by Scribe Design, Gillingham, Kent
Printed and bound in Great Britain at the University Press, Cambridge

# Contents

# Introduction

Tread carefully if you wish to commission a building project. There are many snares for the uninitiated. To obtain an efficient, well-planned and attractive building of lasting value needs a major contribution from you the client. You must devote time and care to deciding exactly what your needs are, and also record them. This record is what is referred to in the construction industry as an architect's brief.

The terms 'brief' and 'briefing' are used in this book, although not understood as such by all the English-speaking world, to be a client's main contribution to the process of building. They are used in Britain and are synonymous with the terms 'program' and 'programming' used in the United States of America.

A brief is everything an architect needs to know about the building a client needs. The client's yearnings, ideas and vision should be clearly expressed in it, together with every activity and important piece of equipment or treasured possession to be accommodated. All has to be thought of and noted down by the client before an acceptable design can be produced. It is more than a verbal exchange of ideas. It is a creative act which shapes the subsequent building and it should be presented in the form of a well-constructed document which is concise, realistic and as comprehensive as possible.

Compiling a brief is a task which few people are sure about. Few know how to go about producing one, or realize its value and importance. After all, the majority of clients are new to the building industry. They are building for the first time, and as first-time clients they cannot be expected to know what briefing is all about.

This book sets out the various steps which clients, architects and consultants usually follow when briefing takes place. It offers a practical stage-by-stage approach to briefing and tries to simplify the procedures and methods which must be faced when setting out to compile a brief. Checklists, flow diagrams and charts are included for ease of reference.

The guidebook offers:

o    A basis for systematic working.

o    A more expansive view of the possibilities and options open to clients.

o    An aide memoire for the more experienced client.

o    An aid for anyone who may wish to reconsider or rethink his usual methods of briefing.

Parts of this book are devoted to seeing from the client's point of view and anticipating the problems which might arise. The client's responsibilities are explained and his role as initiator and contributor to the brief is highlighted. Also, many complicated and involved procedures are interpreted and simplified for the benefit of inexperienced clients by:

o    Suggesting how to organize to tackle the job.

o    Highlighting the most essential steps to take and in what order.

o    Setting out a wide range of points which should be considered in ideal circumstances for best results.

o    Explaining how the different consultants, experts, designers and others involved in construction work relate to each other and the client.

Much guidance and advice has been published in the past for the benefit of clients and their architects. A search of library shelves will produce a variety of guidebooks and official manuals and reports. They each expound the main aspects of briefing, recommend procedures and vital activities not to be overlooked, and attempt to introduce a conventional approach applicable to all projects. Some organizations use highly sophisticated methods and take briefing very seriously, others hardly at all. No generally accepted method applicable to all building projects exists, and first-time clients find themselves at a disadvantage, being innocent of the nature and field of activity they are entering into.

The prime purpose of this book is to help reduce uncertainty and lead the reader away from any preconceptions which he may have about briefing and the part consultants aud contractors play in it. Being designed in sequential form to flow through the evolving stages of the briefing process, it is hoped it will prove easy to refer to and be a support to the daily activities of brief writers, designers and architects.

# Acknowledgements

Perhaps the largest debt of gratitude is owed to the many people who can never be named. Those colleagues I worked with over the years, the people who had massive building programmes to achieve: clients, solicitors, planners, architects, engineers, quantity surveyors, who repeatedly challenged the working methods of the architectural profession. This critical atmosphere continually sharpened my concern about the need for clients to understand what briefing was about and what architects can do for them.

During the life of the Building Research Establishment Advisory Group on *Briefing and Initial Design,* of which I was a member, I gained an insight into how the subject of briefing was regarded by architects and their clients. Witnessing the studies undertaken, and hearing of the experience and conclusions of successful architects and major client groups on the subject, proved to be an invaluable introduction to writing this book – an idea far from my mind at that time. Another formulating experience for me was taking part in one of the group's experiments, doomed to pass quickly into oblivion: the drafting of a small 'primer,' as it was called, in an attempt to produce a concise, informative pocket guide for clients. This objective proved to be quite unrealizable by a committee but I realize now how beneficial it was for me to hear the views of the members of the group, Douglas Smith, John Stillman, Frank Duffy, Tim Poulson, Mike Hacker, Noel O'Reilly of BRE, the two participating clients, D.E. Simmance of Weetabix Limited, M. Robertson of IBM and, not least, Bill White of Building Design Partnership, and I am grateful for this.

Finally a word of thanks to Maritz Vandenburg, Commissioning Editor for The Architectural Press, and Neil Warnock-Smith, Publisher for Butterworth-Heinemann for their encouragement and guidance, and special thanks to my wife Trude and our sons for their continuous support and understanding.

# Preliminary and prebriefing steps

## How to begin to compile a brief

This chapter has been written with a double purpose in mind:
○    To approach the subject of briefing in a way best suited to helping you as client to make an early start on your building project.
○    To suggest positive steps which can be put in hand immediately and which are not detrimental to the future development of your project.

## 1.1    Setting the scene

To set down a brief can be a severely taxing business. An architect or designer beginning work on a project must have instructions and information from the client. Usually, precise details and descriptions of the building required are called for. Most clients are likely to be unclear about what is wanted at the outset. If a first-time client, you could feel overcome by a sense of uncertainty. This is not unusual.

To complicate matters even more, you will find that almost anyone with an interest in the building is likely to offer their own preferences, advice and demands for inclusion in the brief. Apart from colleagues, staff or family, others who will be more than ready to intervene and let their views be known are neighbours, legislators, civic groups and, of course, the building users. Unsolicited contributions of this sort are usually of value but not always helpful. What can be most offputting is the quantity of information offered and its contradictory nature. But there is no need to be concerned about these matters at so early a stage in briefing.

There are numerous procedures and methods of briefing which can be brought into use to help resolve the problems of complication and any surfeit of information. They are not widely known outside the architectural profession. Until clients experience their usefulness, it will not become immediately apparent how these methods bring reassurance and confidence when compiling a brief.

Most newcomers to briefing feel uncertain about what is expected of them, what they should know and what they should do. It is this factor most of all which needs to be resolved if a client is to successfully inform his architect and consultants about the building he needs. A tentative start on the brief by the client is normal and will be expected by most consultants. Unless you are experienced and have commissioned buildings before, it is virtually impossible to set down at the first interview what is required of a building. It might be suggested that a schedule of accommodation be decided and standards like finishes and cost limits be set at the first meeting, at least sufficient for a start to be made on a design. This is the usual expectation. Yet it is in fact not the best way to begin briefing. There are some fundamental points to think carefully about first of all.

## 1.2 Fundamental points to consider

Are you able to decide positively at the outset about your real needs? Can you be sure whether to move to a new location and build new premises, or stay put and refit, or perhaps remodel, renovate and refurnish, or extend in some way? These questions arise at the commencement of most building projects, whatever size or type they happen to be.

It is easy to leap instinctively into making a choice before conducting further studies and investigations. Failing to consider fully the matters of location and the need to build afresh, can mean that important factors are ignored which are vital to the success of your building when brought into use.

Set out below are matters which need to be studied closely by the client, his advisors and his professional consultants:

o    Are we well informed about the present activities of our organization and those who are to use the building?

o    Do we have an idea about possible growth in the future?

o    Are we satisfied about the location of the premises, taking into

**Fig 1.1**

First steps before deciding to build

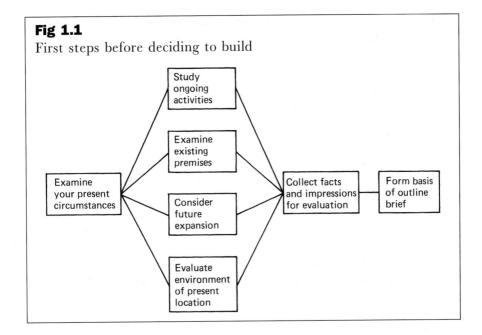

account the activities of neighbours, the prevailing atmospheric conditions and proximity of airports, railway lines, roads, chimneys and similar features? This applies to both new and existing locations.

o     Do we know sufficient about future development plans of a local authority, government agency or neighbouring property owner? Do they affect our building, its site or the locality, for good or bad?

o     Do we know whether our present building meets the needs of the organization, or family, its occupants and visitors?

o     Have we looked at these questions carefully enough?

To make a choice involves avoiding guesswork and being as realistic and factual as possible. It is important not to choose solutions when considering basic needs, for example opting for a new extension before assessing how the existing building is used and whether it is underused or causes problems of some kind. Even if it has recently been built and occupied, the short experience of the occupiers is bound to suggest some shortcomings which need to be taken account of. Older buildings are very often found to have been constraining the activities of an organization, or burdening it with excessive maintenance or running costs.

So the first useful step to take involves getting better acquainted with your present building, how it is used, and how it suits you. This also applies to those who are in temporary accommodation or rented property. It is an essential but salutory exercise which need not take up a great deal of time.

## 1.3    Appraisals – getting better acquainted with a building

No one knows the faults in a building better than those using it. Most people can point to deficiencies in the roof, plumbing or ventilation. But how easy is it to find out whether those using the building are subjected to unnecessary stress or inconvenience? How many people are aware that the environment produced by a building makes a big contribution to their sense of wellbeing? And how many feel they can evaluate it properly?

When a building is designed, subtleties of atmosphere can he created to enhance the experience of the occupier. Interiors can take on a surprisingly large range of different qualities. Good design is not just a question of good taste or fashion, or creating an impact. Appearances are deceptive, however pleasing or depressing they may seem to be. The form and composition of the fabric of a building – the more permanent aspects of it – are the root elements affecting its influence on those using it. The key factors which need assessment are:

o     Room sizes and shapes, their relationship to others; their aspect and outlook.

o     Movement patterns, checking whether corridor routes and positions of lifts and staircases are satisfactory.

o     Flexibility; and facility for extension.

o     Insulation against loss of heat, ingress of noise.

o     Permanency of the building in its setting (whether it is a listed building or not).

o     Suitability of the site and its environs; its general acceptability to owner and users alike.

A proforma is set out on p. 5 to help with the assessment of these points. It uses your existing accommodation as a prompt to bring out how you regard a building in use. This will help by sharpening the perception, encouraging critical thought about buildings and stimulating a feeling of what is needed. It must be stressed that this exercise is not directed at the reshaping or improving of one's present building.

There is no need to answer the questions listed in the proforma in a detailed manner; merely write down the various impressions you have after looking at your existing premises. What will prove useful later in the briefing process are your spontaneous impressions, or those of any others who may be helping with this task. These impressions are very important because:

o     They help set standards in a client's mind and alert him to examine all sorts of aspects about buildings, which in time brings about a good awareness of what is really needed.

## Prebriefing proforma

Activities – How is your building used?

1. *Spaces – Rooms – Halls: are they overcrowded?*
   - Is the furniture and equipment spaced too close together?
   - Is there any clutter which encroaches on the space or other areas adjoining?
   - Are stores considered large enough?
   - Do stores contain items which are out of date, damaged or no longer required?
   - Are any rooms obviously too small?
   - Do some room shapes seem unsuitable to you?

2. *Which of your existing rooms suit you?*
   - Note down the features of rooms which you have proved to be ideal for your purposes: size – shape – aspect – other features.

3. *Are any spaces underused or unpopular? If so, why?*
   - Because of bad natural light or outlook?
   - Because of inadequate heating?
   - No longer needed?
   - Wrongly located in relation to other rooms?
   - Any other reasons?

4. *Service rooms: lavatories, kitchens and bathrooms: are they properly equipped?*
   - Are fittings or equipment out of date?
   - Do they fall short of statutory requirements?
   - Are they up to the standard *you* would prefer?
   - Are lavatories or kitchens accommodating items which properly should be kept in a storeroom?

5. *Circulation: is it adequate?*
   - Is there enough space between and around items of furniture, equipment, fittings, etc.?
   - Are corridor widths adequate?
   - Do door widths or door swings restrict the movement of equipment or wheelchairs?
   - Are there points where busy circulation routes clash? Is there congestion at any point?
   - Do you think your present corridors are too long?
   - Are some rooms spaced a great distance apart?
   - Do you think your present staircases cause difficulties for some of the people using them (too narrow – too steep – other reason)?
   - Is there a tendency to avoid moving to rooms on other floor levels, up or down?
   - Do you have a lift? Would you prefer a lift?

6. *Existing site's environmental standards*
   - Are the buildings and spaces surrounding your property a nuisance to you and your activities?
   - Define any problems you find (noise – smell – appearance – restrictions).
   - Are there traffic problems (either generally in the area or on your site) for those visiting your property? For deliveries, parking, garaging, etc.?
   - Consider the possibility of obtaining better conditions at a new location; set down the various points you would change about your present site if it were possible.

*See Section 1.4 for appraisal of new site.*

o      They display the client's preferences and observations, which when examined later contribute much that is useful for collecting into the brief.
o      They help the client to present realistic requirements to an architect and any other consultants involved when briefing commences.

This exercise is a vital contribution to the work done by an architect when appraising a building or working up a brief with a client. However, it must not be confused with the work carried out when a professional appraises the qualities and condition of a particular building. He will conduct a highly detailed study and closely examine all aspects of the building in a critical manner. This process demands far more skill and experience than a client organization would normally possess. Facts and technical details need to be established precisely and recorded accurately. It is then that professional people should be consulted. Their experience, advice and skill becomes a necessity.

### 1.3.1  Appraisal of existing buildings

When looking at existing property with a view to altering or reshaping it, to follow an ordered sequence of events can be beneficial. One method of study is set out in Fig 1.2. When applied, it brings some clarity to the otherwise vague and unsubstantiated claims people might make about using the building.

To illustrate how simple it is to use this sequence, it is applied below to a problem which is experienced in many large educational buildings.

### *Example: appraisal of high school teaching accommodation*

*1. Inception*
o      Problem: the headmaster claims that he has difficulty in allocating appropriate teaching spaces to the subjects being taught at the time they were needed.
o      Objective: to prove the validity of his claim, and to discover what extensions and alterations were needed to ease the problem.
o      End product: a report for presentation to a policy-making group (client committee or school governors).

*2. Feasibility*
The following is a tentative theoretical approach to solving the problem.

The architect knew from the education authority's professional sources that the intake of pupils predicted in future years required an organization of nine streams of children between the ages of 12 and 18 (a nine-form entry mixed comprehensive school). Information about

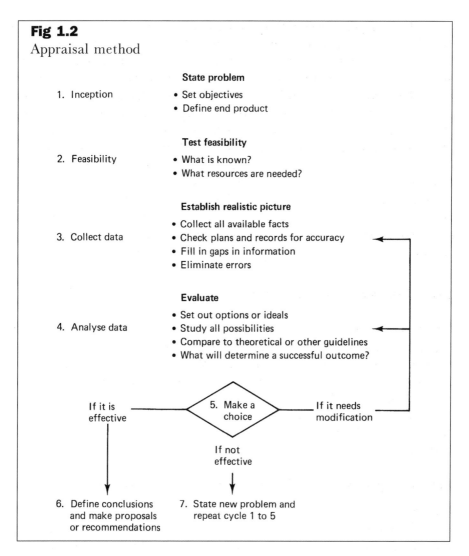

**Fig 1.2**
Appraisal method

| | **State problem** |
|---|---|
| 1. Inception | • Set objectives |
| | • Define end product |

| | **Test feasibility** |
|---|---|
| 2. Feasibility | • What is known? |
| | • What resources are needed? |

| | **Establish realistic picture** |
|---|---|
| | • Collect all available facts |
| 3. Collect data | • Check plans and records for accuracy |
| | • Fill in gaps in information |
| | • Eliminate errors |

| | **Evaluate** |
|---|---|
| | • Set out options or ideals |
| 4. Analyse data | • Study all possibilities |
| | • Compare to theoretical or other guidelines |
| | • What will determine a successful outcome? |

If it is effective — 5. Make a choice — If it needs modification

If not effective

6. Define conclusions and make proposals or recommendations

7. State new problem and repeat cycle 1 to 5

the curriculum and staff numbers was available together with a method of translating them into a schedule of variously mixed spaces, tailored to suit the subjects taught. Resources needed were an education professional advisor and an architect/researcher to work on the theoretical conclusions and produce an outline brief, and a project architect, building economist and environmental engineer to appraise the building with the outline brief in mind. Also the occasional involvement of the client's liaison officer was necessary.

*3. Data collection*
Up-to-date measured floor plans and engineering installation drawings were on file (microfilm records).

The architect visited the school with the client's liaison officer to mark up the plans to show the current use of space as presently existing (which differs from the original brief and design intentions).

A comprehensive property condition survey was compiled which included all aspects of the school: the quality of the structure, engineering installations, internal finishes, and also the external elements, such as pavings, boundaries and drainage. Reference to the client's property survey records and a number of on-site surveys were needed.

### 4. Analysis

The education professional adviser compared the theoretical results setting out the ideal space requirements with the headteacher's ideas about the teaching areas he needed. Then the form and arrangement of the school buildings was examined by the architect to test how the new space requirements would fit into the existing structure and where an extension might best be sited. Also the results of the property condition survey were studied to discover what life the existing structure had, and whether it could be improved to extend its remaining life.

Analysis showed the headteacher to be correct. The school was planned in such a way that more than the theoretical minimum teaching area is required to support the school organization.

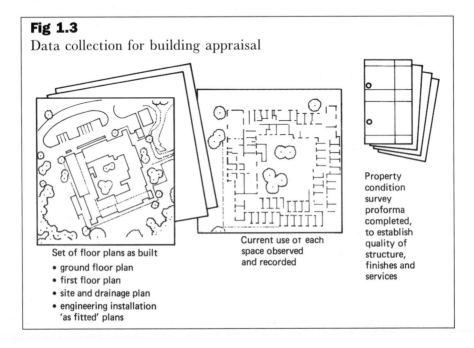

### Fig 1.3
Data collection for building appraisal

Set of floor plans as built
• ground floor plan
• first floor plan
• site and drainage plan
• engineering installation 'as fitted' plans

Current use ot each space observed and recorded

Property condition survey proforma completed, to establish quality of structure, finishes and services

## An outline property condition survey procedure

1. List all main elements of the building, i.e.

| | |
|---|---|
| Roof | Ceilings |
| External walling | Internal walls |
| External doors | Internal doors |
| Pavings | Flooring |
| etc. | etc. |

2. Assess the physical condition of these elements. Use categories such as:

| Category condition | Definition |
|---|---|
| *Good* | Good as new. |
| *Reasonable* | Very satisfactory, not likely to need attention for many years. |
| *Tolerable* | Generally good overall and working as intended and not requiring attention in the short term. |
| *Part poor* | Generally adequate but requiring minor repairs or partial replacement. |
| *Part bad* | In very bad condition in parts only. |
| *Bad* | Generally in very bad condition – requiring immediate attention. |

3. Note age of structure and its parts.

4. Search records to discover whether there have been any serious structural problems in the life of the building, particularly with the foundations and drains.

5. Establish if the structure falls short of modern standards.

6. Assess: (a) cost of bringing the building up to an 'as new' state, including the work needed to conform to the Building Regulations etc., (b) expected life of the structure after improvement.

## Fig 1.4

Examples of forms used for property condition surveys (reproduced with permission of Cheshire County Council); see also Appendix A

**MECHANICAL SERVICES**  SH SPACE HEATING

(including heat generation)
Gas ☐ Oil ☐ Coal ☐ Elect. ☐ Other ☐

| MAIN COMPONENTS — WATER | Code | Cat. | % |
|---|---|---|---|
| Air handling/Air Conditioning Systems | SH 5101 | | |
| Fan Convectors systems | SH 5105 | | |
| Natural Convector systems | SH 5109 | | |
| Radiator systems | SH 5113 | | |
| Floor coil system | SH 5117 | | |
| Ceiling system | SH 5121 | | |
| Others | SH 5125 | | |

| MAIN COMPONENTS — ELECTRICITY | | | |
|---|---|---|---|
| Under Floor/coiling system | SH 6101 | | |

Thermal

On Peal

FISC CODE    BLOCK NO.

BLOCK REF NO.

| CONSTRUCTION TYPE | | ISSUING OFFICER No. | |
|---|---|---|---|

| AREA | | YEAR OF CONST. | |
|---|---|---|---|

DIVISION

YEAR OF SURVEY

**DC DOMESTIC COLD WATER (CONT.)**

| Tank Cold Water inc. tanks | DC 1446 | |
|---|---|---|
| | | 100 |

| SUBSIDIARY COMPONENTS | Code | Cat. |
|---|---|---|
| Tank (cistern) | DC 1451 | |
| Pipework | DC 1456 | |

**INTERIOR ELEMENT**
CE CEILINGS

MAIN COMPONENTS

Plastered surfaces

Boarding or accoustic tiling

Proprietary Suspended ceiling

Exposed woodwool slabs/stra

Exposed metal decking

SUBSIDIARY COMPO

Rooflight linings

Exposed structural member

FL FLOORING

MAIN COMPONENTS

Wood Block inc. skirtings,

Granwood inc. skirtings, e

T & G Strip Boarding inc.

Concrete/grano/stone inc

Ceramic/Quarry Tiles inc

Terrazzo Tiles inc. skirtir

Lino/P.V.C. sheet inc. sl

Lino/P.V.C. tiles inc. ski

Carpet inc. skirtings, et

Pitch Mastic Screeding

SUBSIDIARY CO

Skirtings

Matwells

Floor channels and t

IW INTERNAL V

MAIN COMPON

Exposed Brickwork

Exposed Blockwor

Plastered surface

Plasterboard dry l

Wall tiling/glazed

Specialist or glaz

SUBSIDIARY

Balustrades and

ID INTERN.

**EXTERIOR ELEMENTS**
RO ROOFING

| MAIN COMPONENTS | Code | Cat | % |
|---|---|---|---|
| Felt flat inc. perimeter treatment, drainage, etc. | RO 1101 | | |
| Asphalt inc. perimeter treatment, drainage, etc. | RO 1103 | | |
| Sheet lead inc. perimeter treatment, drainage | RO 1105 | | |
| Slates inc. flashings, verges, drainage, etc. | RO 1107 | | |
| Clay or conc. tiles, inc. verges, drainage, etc. | RO 1109 | | |
| Asbestos slates, inc. flashings, verges, drainage | RO 1111 | | |
| Metal sheeting inc. flashings, drainage, etc. | RO 1113 | | |
| Asbestos sheeting inc. flashings, drainage, etc. | RO 1115 | | |
| Felt pitched inc. perimeter treatment, drainage, etc. | RO 1117 | | |
| | | | 100 |

| SUBSIDIARY COMPONENTS | Code | Cat. |
|---|---|---|
| Metal flashings | RO 1119 | |
| Upstands and edge trims (flat roof) | RO 1121 | |
| Valley gutters (pitched roofs) | RO 1401 | |
| Metal rainwater gutters and fall pipes | RO 1406 | |
| PVC rainwater gutters and fall pipes | RO 1411 | |
| Asbestos rainwater gutters and fall pipes | RO 1416 | |
| Rooflights, patent glazing and roof windows | RO 1123 | |

**EW EXTERNAL WALLING**

| MAIN COMPONENTS | Code | Cat | % |
|---|---|---|---|
| Brickwork inc. parapet walls, chimneys, etc. | EW 1125 | | |
| Blockwork inc. parapet walls, chimneys, etc. | EW 1127 | | |
| Stonework inc. parapet walls, chimneys, etc. | EW 1129 | | |
| Rendered surfaces | EW 1131 | | |
| Slate/Tile hanging inc. flashings, trims, etc. | EW 1133 | | |
| Timber cladding, inc. flashings, trims, etc. | EW 1135 | | |
| Concrete frame and/or concrete cladding | EW 1001 | | |
| Timber curtain walling inc. infil panels, etc. | EW 1137 | | |
| Steel curtain walling inc. infil panels, etc. | EW 1139 | | |
| Aluminium curtain walling inc. infil panels, etc. | EW 1141 | | |
| Plastic coated curtain walling inc. infil panels | EW 1143 | | |
| Timber windows inc. sub. cills and ironmongery | EW 1145 | | |
| Steel windows inc. sub. cills and ironmongery | EW 1147 | | |
| Aluminium windows inc. sub. cills and ironmongery | EW 1149 | | |
| P.V.C. windows inc. sub. cills and ironmongery | EW 1151 | | |
| | | | 100 |

FISC CODE    BLOCK NO.

BLOCK REF NO.

| CONSTRUCTION TYPE | | ISSUING OFFICER No. | |
|---|---|---|---|

| AREA | | YEAR OF CONST. | |
|---|---|---|---|

DIVISION

YEAR OF SURVEY

**EW EXTERNAL WALLING (CONT.)**

| SUBSIDIARY COMPONENTS | Code | Cat. |
|---|---|---|
| Parapet walls/copings. | EW 1153 | |
| Chimneys | EW 1155 | |
| Infil panels | EW 1157 | |
| Sub cills surrounds (stone, slate, asbestos, tiled) | EW 1159 | |
| Ironmongery (window fastenings, hinges, etc.) | EW 1161 | |
| Draught proofing (integral/applied) | EW 7101 | |
| Bedding and pointing to glazing | EW 1163 | |
| Fire Escapes inc. balustrades | EW 1165 | |

**ED EXTERNAL DOORS**

| MAIN COMPONENTS | Code | Cat. | % |
|---|---|---|---|
| Softwood inc. frames and ironmongery | ED 1167 | | |
| Hardwood inc. frames and ironmongery | ED 1169 | | |
| Steel inc. frames and ironmongery | ED 1171 | | |
| Aluminium inc. frames and ironmongery | ED 1173 | | |
| Roller Shutters inc. frames and ironmongery | ED 1175 | | |
| Sliding folding inc. frames and ironmongery | ED 1177 | | |
| | | | 100 |

| SUBSIDIARY COMPONENTS | Code | Cat. |
|---|---|---|
| Ironmongery | ED 1179 | |
| Draught proofing (integral/applied) | ED 7111 | |

**E P EXTERNAL DECORATION**

| Overall decoration | EP 1301 | | 100 |
|---|---|---|---|

| SUBSIDIARY COMPONENTS | Code | Cat. |
|---|---|---|
| Timber windows and doors — painted | EP 1305 | |
| Timber windows and doors — varnished | EP 1309 | |
| Timber windows and doors — treated preservative | EP 1313 | |
| Steel windows and doors — painted | EP 1317 | |
| Wall surfaces — painted | EP 1321 | |
| Timber generally — painted | EP 1325 | |
| Timber generally — treated preservative | EP 1329 | |

| MAIN COMPONENTS | | | |
|---|---|---|---|
| Softwood, inc. linings, etc. and ironmongery | ID 1282 | | |
| Hardwood inc. linings, etc. and ironmongery | ID 1285 | | |

| Laboratory Fittings | | |
|---|---|---|
| General Fittings | FF 1385 | |

*5. Consideration of options*

o       Reorganize the interior arrangement to provide a more accessible and workable relationship of spaces and avoid extending the building at all.

o       Demolish those parts of the building in a bad state of repair and expensive to heat. Reorganize the remaining parts of the building and add on modest extensions.

At this stage the architect would need to illustrate with diagrams and architectural sketches various schemes of modification and extension. These sketches would be of use in producing cost comparisons of the options available.

*6. Conclusions and proposals*

Conclusions could be:

o       The headteacher's claims are justified and improvements are needed.

o       An improvement project based on the first option would be proposed for immediate attention by the school governors and local authority.

o       Some upgrading of the building fabric should be carried out.

When preparing a report about a building appraisal of this kind, it would be natural to structure it to coincide with the six divisions of this method study.

### 1.3.2   Appraisals for the home owner seeking to extend

A home owner wishing to build an extension would, at the very least, consult a valuer and consider very carefully the needs of his family in terms of space required. Minimal considerations could be:

o       Ascertain the present value of the house as if it were to be put on the market.

o       Ask what it would realize if sold with the proposed extension completed. This establishes whether investment on the extension would add an equivalent amount to the value of the house.

o       If the proposal does not add to the value of the house, find out why. Would the enlarged house be situated in an area which would not attract buyers of the type of property you will be creating? Is the existing house below accepted standards? For example, it may have an old-fashioned plan, high maintenance costs or unusual architecture.

Obtaining factual answers to these questions will help the owner decide if it really suits him and his family, practically and financially.

Whatever the finding might be, and possibly in spite of negative results, it may be decided that the house as built in its environment is quite acceptable. Then the proposals about adaptations and extension need close scrutiny. Consulting an architect briefly would help with deliberations about the ideas which come first to mind, and bring out any faulty reasoning or unfounded assumptions.

Considerations would very likely include the following key points:

o      To predict increases in the rateable value and running costs, water rate, and heating and lighting costs, and decide whether they are acceptable or not.

o      To check whether the existing services are adequate, for example:
—    Output of central heating boiler.
—    Size of water storage tanks and incoming mains.
—    Whether the drainage system is low enough in the ground to accept additional branches without the need for some reconstruction.

o      To ascertain whether the proposed extension would diminish the quality and usefulness of the existing rooms, perhaps affecting view, daylighting, sunlight or neighbours.

o      To ascertain whether any deficiencies which the valuer might have found can be improved and whether the improvements can be included in the project at minimal cost.

At the end of a simple study of this kind, the client could find there was a different, less obvious scheme of adaptation or extension which suited him better. Looking squarely at any deficiencies and envisaging the consequences of changing the house can awaken a keener sense of the relative values of the plan, its arrangement and various features. Qualities of the house not clearly seen before are highlighted and the proposed improvements can then be more effectively weighed in relation to them.

## 1.4    Site selection and appraisal

Far too often the architect is faced with a site already chosen by the client, possibly already purchased. Afterwards, rushed by pressure of time and economics, the architect works to realize an effective building which relates well to the site and its surroundings. Skilful fusion of the site and the buildings placed on it is the objective he strives for, but the quality and degree of success of a project depend basically on the intrinsic quality and character of the site itself. Any major deficiencies inherent in the land, its shape or relationship to its surroundings and other buildings can rarely be remedied when the building is designed. It is worthwhile devoting time and energy to carefully selecting a site most appropriate to the project in mind. With advice from his consultants, the client must:

o      Determine the site requirements for his project.
o      Weigh the relative merits of alternative sites.

o    Become knowledgeable about all features of the chosen site and their relative importance as an influence on the proposed use of the land.

### Searching for a site: a method

*First*, try to draw up a list of the points which you consider most important about the site you would like, such as:

o    Site area.
o    Preferred location.
o    Ideal shape.
o    Maximum variation in ground levels.

A starting point is essential and some estimate must be made in order to pinpoint possible sites. Quite correctly, this task leads to thinking about the size of the building required. So a start has to be made on drawing up the brief for the building itself.

*Second*, reconnoitre. Examine the territory in the region or locality you are most interested in. Aids to finding possible sites are:

o    Ordnance survey maps.
o    Road maps.
o    County or district plans showing planning zones.
o    Aerial photographs.
o    Chamber of Commerce publications.
o    Town street maps and local publicity literature.
o    Local authority promotional literature.

Investigations of likely areas and tracts of land must ultimately be done on foot, but much useful data relating to each site can be collected from maps, booklets and photographs.

After narrowing down the choices to a reasonably short list, begin a careful analysis of each one by noting down and comparing their features, both favourable and unfavourable, and assessing their potential.

When carrying out a comparative analysis, the experience gained can often lead to a questioning of what were originally thought to be acceptable criteria. In spite of there being a systematic process, those involved might develop a feeling or hunch that a particular site is preferable to the others. If this happens, reviewing the features and favourable points noted down for this site could reveal various aspects which, whilst diverging from the criteria originally set, can turn out to offer an ideal opportunity to the architect to produce an ideal design solution.

To aid in the selection between the shortlist of possible sites, a planning consultant or an architect could help to clarify which criteria are valid and most advantageous.

Obviously, the ideal site is the one which, with least modification, best suits the project in mind. Modifying negative features or compensating for lack of services can mean that extensive site development

## Checklist of points to consider when examining a site

| Item | Source | Recording of data |
|------|--------|-------------------|
| **1. Physical details – General** | | |
| • Location of plot.<br>• Shape of plot.<br>• Superficial area inside boundaries.<br>• Ground levels, depressions. | • Ordnance survey sheets and topographical survey, plotted to scale, with spot levels and/or contour lines added. | • Site location plan showing surroundings.<br>• General site survey plan with boundaries and all physical features shown. |
| **2. Some features to look for**<br><br>*Features at ground level or below it*<br><br>*Investigate:*<br>• Character of subsoils.<br>• Level of ground water.<br>• Excess or lack of topsoil.<br>• Methane gas pockets. | • Trial holes or bore holes; mineral record plans. | • Cross-sectional drawings taken through site. |
| *Check for existence of:*<br>• Filled-in ground, filled- or covered-in basements, silted-up watercourses.<br>• Old foundations.<br>• Disused wells, mine shafts, abandoned storage tanks or other sealed-up cavities.<br>• Drainage culverts, underground streams, unknown electricity cable or gas pipe runs.<br>• Disused, existing or proposed mining operations.<br>• Public rights-of-way. | • Old ordnance sheets, local authority records, conveyance plans (part of deeds of sale of land). | • Plot on to general 'as existing' site plan. |

## Checklist of points to consider when examining a site (continued)

| Item | Source | Recording of data |
|---|---|---|
| **Features standing on the site** | | |
| *Investigate:* | | |
| ● Character and quality of any buildings; boundary walls, fences, railings and gates; retaining walls and embankments; trees and plantations. | ● Physical survey and any existing plans belonging to owner or lodged with local authority. | ● Plot on to general 'as existing' site plan. ● Draw up separate plans of buildings. |
| *Check for existence of:* | | |
| ● Overhead power cables or telephone lines. ● Tree-preservation orders. ● Quality of agricultural ground. | ● Site survey and reference to local authority planning department's records. | ● Plot on or endorse general 'as existing' site plan. |
| **Features existing off site** | | |
| *Establish off-site services:* | | |
| ● Drainage connection points for sewage and rainwater, or septic tanks. ● Water service mains. ● Gas service mains. ● Electricity service cables and transformer equipment. ● Telephone and other communication cable runs. | ● Enquire at each undertaking for routes and data on existing or projected utility services, gas and water pressures, power capacities, and drainage runs and depths, from local authority technical departments. | |
| *Establish other off-site influences:* | | |
| ● Ground levels. ● Noise nuisance from neighbouring properties, airports, roads and railways. ● Odours, industrial smells and emissions. ● Approach roads and car parks in vicinity. ● Easements, rights of way. ● Zoning restrictions improvement, and building lines. | ● Existing or projected development may produce problems. Research and advice from experienced consultants is essential. | |

works are needed, and these can add considerably to the building costs, or even require some adjustment to the boundaries. The checklist on pp. 14–15 suggests items which a comparative investigation should take account of. A range of possibilities is set out, not all of which could possibly affect one site. However, they illustrate the kind of problems which could lie undiscovered under, or in the vicinity of, the site; problems which could take time to rectify before site operations could commence. At the very least, they would add to the basic costs of the building project. Hence the need to fully probe and completely survey all aspects of the site before agreeing to acquire it.

When a site is acquired for development, these additional features and influences become an important part of the brief; and are usually found by the architect to be a constraint on his design possibilities. To fail to look closely at a site is foolhardy. Unnecessary complications can occur when discoveries are made after a site is purchased, causing disappointment, sometimes requiring amendment of design or working drawings and usually adding extra cost to the project.

It is vital to know about the existence of adverse influences, such as the lack of gas services or the need to install a pump house to lift sewage to a much shallower outfall sewer, when assessing the development costs of a number of sites. The sooner factual information is obtained about hidden problems, the better. Knowledge of ground conditions, or any undesirable off-site threat to the environmental quality of the site and the projected building, is a necessary aid to realistically comparing alternative sites, and to establishing reasonably accurate estimates of the costs of developing each one.

Furthermore, the information gathered about the site which is chosen is a valuable part of the brief for the building which is to be erected upon it.

## 1.5    Who will help?

### 1.5.1    Engaging consultants

When thinking about what is needed and examining the features of your existing site, or when looking first at a new site, it is not too soon to seek help from experts. There is little one can do when acquiring new property without advice from a bank manager or financial expert. Similarly, to be sure of some clarity when weighing one aspect of a building or site against another, the participation of other experts is helpful. It aids the obtaining of a fuller background to the problem, widens the field of choice, and points to viable and often new ideas to work on. The decisions, of course, finally rest with the client, but expert opinion based on experience and sound practice is invaluable, however small the project.

But who does one approach, and how is it done?

### 1.5.2    Procurement of professional services

It is possible to obtain preliminary advice during the first stages of a project without becoming committed to any particular consultant. Short discussions can be set up, or commissions given for surveys or for limited exploratory studies. This is a sensible approach and good preparation for settling the extent and character of a project. Of course, whilst working with the professional people chosen, opportunities are created for assessing the value of their participation and any contribution they can make to the project you have in mind.

For example, when acquiring a site or existing building, the roles of an estate agent and solicitor are familiar enough. What is perhaps not so well known is the value of the advice a valuation surveyor, architect, structural engineer or building economist can give.

The skills which each profession offers are set out on pp. 18–19 for ease of reference. At first sight you may get the impression that all are equally necessary. However, if you approach various consultants to obtain their views about your project it will be possible to assess which suits your requirements best.

To obtain the best and most appropriate professional services, and build up a truly balanced team of consultants when more than one is required, is a matter of individual judgement and preference. Obvious methods are to:

o    Follow up a personal recommendation.
o    Study advertising literature.
o    Ask professional institutions for assistance.

However, there is much more that can be done. Section 2.7 explores the techniques available in more detail.

It is not suggested that the various consultants indicated be asked for advice on a competitive basis. Each can offer special advice about how to develop a first idea into something feasible. Each would expect the client to consult other experts, either independently or through the architect or project manager. All will contribute something of value to the compiling of an initial brief, and assist in presenting facts and opinions which can help the client formulate the main factors which require a decision. All will suggest consulting some of the other professions if a large project is envisaged.

## Professional services available at preliminary stage for short consultations, commissions, feasibility studies and surveys

| Profession | Special skills |
|---|---|
| Architect | ● The ability to judge the capacity of a building shell, or the adequacy and usefulness of a site.<br>● Will highlight potentiality and snags.<br>● Can illustrate the form of development which is possible.<br>● Conducts a survey of the site or building, and reports on constraints, difficulties and advantages. |
| Valuation surveyor | ● Calculates economic potential of site or building.<br>● Reports on quality of building or site and its value. |
| Building economist (or quantity surveyor) | ● Forecasts costs of project: site works, construction or fitting-out costs, fees and all other likely expenses.<br>● Advises on and prepares costs-in-use studies.<br>● Advises on contracting methods, improvement grants, market trends in the locality and climate of tendering.<br>● Evaluates various options in financial terms. |
| Builder or contractor | ● Offers advice on structural possibilities on the basis of the capability of his firm and the construction techniques he is experienced or specialized in. |
| Structural engineer | ● Initiates, controls and reports on subsoil investigations, quality of natural foundation.<br>● Surveys and reports on the condition and life-expectancy of building and engineering structures.<br>● Provides structural advice and calculations to assist other consultants with reports, appraisals, feasibility studies or sketch ideas. |
| Building surveyor | ● Surveys and reports on the condition and life-expectancy of building materials, components and fittings.<br>● Prepares repair and maintenance programmes and evaluates improvement and ongoing maintenance costs. |
| Services engineer | ● Provides environmental advice: surveys and reports on the condition and life-expectancy of heating, ventilation, electrical, gas and other installations; also lifts, water supply and special engineering installations. |

**Professional services available at preliminary stage for short consultations, commissions, feasibility studies and surveys (continued)**

| Profession | Special skills |
|---|---|
| | ● Prepares repair and maintenance programmes and evaluates ongoing maintenance costs.<br>● Suggests energy conservation measures to adopt. |
| Landscape architect, forestry | ● Surveys condition of trees, ponds, and other planting; reports on how site, property or adjoining owners may be affected.<br>● Highlights potential for landscaping, benefiting client and neighbourhood, and for conserving existing features of value. |
| Town planner | ● Advises on probable outcome of development proposal, change of use, or new development.<br>● Interprets planning law.<br>● Prepares development plans, diagrams, designs for large-scale schemes embracing a number of buildings, or for highly sensitive central area site. |
| Estate agent | ● Advises on potentialities for sale of property to be vacated.<br>● Suggests alterations or improvements to property to assist with sale or enhance its value. |

*General services which all professions will very likely offer*

● To assist in defining and compiling a brief.
● To manage the project, calling on expert advice and assistance from consultants of other disciplines.
● To act as an agent in obtaining outline planning permission.
● Sometimes a project manager can be approached at this stage to say how he or she would organize the contributions of all the expert opinions required.

### 1.5.3 Professional fees

At this time you will want to know how much it might cost to engage an architect or other consultant. Each professional institution provides advisory booklets describing how their members are expected to calculate their fees and when to make their charges. These are specially provided for clients. If referred to before meeting a consultant, they can help you prepare questions about anything you do not quite understand.

At the first meeting, time should be spent discussing your requirements and assessing whether they can be realized within your budget. Although fees take up a relatively small part of the total cost of a project, they very much reflect the character and type of services your project needs and these must be established and agreed before the cost of professional fees can be ascertained.

Help and advice given during the preliminary stages of a project would most likely be charged on an hourly basis. For short exploratory studies or surveys the client should establish the hourly rate to be charged and obtain some indication of a possible overall cost before agreeing to continue. Many of the services set out on pp. 18–19 might be charged in this way.

On the other hand, the costs of the more extensive architectural services needed for the design and supervision of a full building project are calculated as a percentage of the construction costs involved. The actual percentage can vary considerably depending on the project cost and the complexity of the building type. Also, if substantial engineering or other specialist services are to be given, these would be additional charges calculated in a similar way.

Determining these costs with any degree of accuracy at so early a stage is virtually impossible. It is only when the type of building work to be undertaken becomes clear at initial brief stage that any assessment should be attempted. If a rough estimate is acceptable, then reference to the additional material included in Section 2.9 will help build up a very broad picture of the costs involved.

### 1.6    Making speedy progress

The wish or pressing need to get on with a project of whatever kind can foster a sense of impatience. Stopping to consider other options and seek the opinions and advice of others can seem a negative thing to do. There are costs involved: professional fees and the investment of valuable time. There is also the feeling that there may be an unnecessary delay in bringing the project to fruition. 'Why hesitate?', the client may ask.

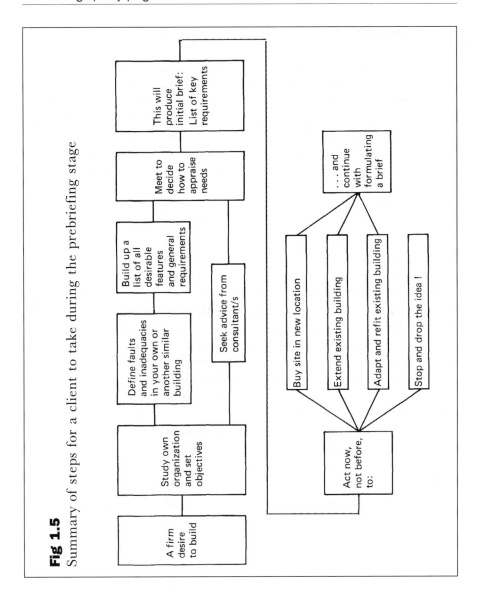

**Fig 1.5**
Summary of steps for a client to take during the prebriefing stage

It is not a matter of being overcautious. Unless already experienced in briefing and working with consultants and contractors, the
client is unlikely to be knowledgeable enough about how to write a brief
and instruct the designers and contractors so that he gets the results
he envisages.

As the client, he holds a basic idea in his mind, an idea which is
to be developed through the activities of designers into a form which
can be realized in a building. He needs to know how this happens and
how to keep control of the process. Preliminary consultations assist in

the first stages of expanding the basic ideas into an initial brief. They provide:

○     A clearer view of the project, its nature, size and value – to know more precisely what you are aiming at.

○     Good knowledge of the character of the site, or building to be altered, with details of the environment – to know where you are going to be located.

○     First ideas about the particular consultants to engage on the project – to know who to have working with you, and which professions.

## 1.7     Summary

This chapter has been written with a double purpose in mind:

○     To approach the subject of briefing in a way best suited to helping a client make an early start on a building project.

○     To suggest positive steps which can be put in hand immediately and which are not detrimental to the future development of the project. However, do not press on too far with the initial investigations, or firm up on the ideas you have about your project, or begin to implement them, before consulting other chapters of this book. Certainly those acting as clients for the first time – or who have personnel in their organization who have little or no experience in briefing – should examine Chapters 2–6 before making a serious start on compiling a brief, or appointing consultants.

# Who are the people involved?

**Finding out more about how architects, consultants and contractors are organized and how they relate to each other will help you to choose the people best suited to work with**

This chapter will help you to:

○     Decide which consultant to approach first.

○     Identify the professional services which will suit you or your organization best.

○     Begin working confidently with the consultants you have selected on your building project.

Have you a clear impression of those who take part in a project, who they are and what they do? To be unsure about the identity and function of the people you meet, whether they are in groups or acting as individuals, can undermine a project right from the start.

Every building project, whatever its nature, involves three main groups of people. Each has a distinct role and depends on the others. The three groups are:

○     Those with an idea who promote and instruct – the clients.

○     Those who design and think out the form and composition of the project – the designers.

○     Those who construct the building – the contractors.

Few individuals or organizations are conscious of the role a client plays in a construction project. Usually they are not fully aware of how a client relates to designers and contractors, or aware of the relationships with the various other people and outside organizations who become involved in a building project.

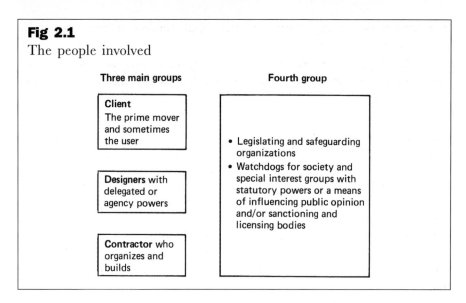

**Fig 2.1**
The people involved

**Three main groups**

**Client**
The prime mover
and sometimes
the user

**Designers** with
delegated or
agency powers

**Contractor** who
organizes and
builds

**Fourth group**

- Legislating and safeguarding
  organizations
- Watchdogs for society and
  special interest groups with
  statutory powers or a means
  of influencing public opinion
  and/or sanctioning and
  licensing bodies

All outsiders of this sort should be thought of as a separate group because, whilst not strictly part of the project team, they exist largely as an influence to be contended with, and usually intrude in some way into every project. This fourth group must not be overlooked. It includes all those who legislate and safeguard the interests of the locality and enforce codes of building and other regulations.

Sometimes, because of the nature of the firms or organizations involved, only two main groups seem to be involved. These are simply rearrangements of the three basic functional groups. Examples are shown in Fig 2.2.

Although appearances suggest otherwise, clients with in-house designers, or contractors offering a design-build service, are really not

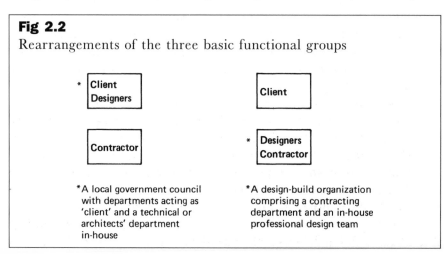

**Fig 2.2**
Rearrangements of the three basic functional groups

\* **Client**
**Designers**

**Contractor**

**Client**

\* **Designers**
**Contractor**

\*A local government council
with departments acting as
'client' and a technical or
architects' department
in-house

\*A design-build organization
comprising a contracting
department and an in-house
professional design team

a homogeneous group. They are two separate but related parts of a corporate or larger body.

In the next few pages the various types of organizational groups which make up the client, designer and contracting groups are looked at more closely.

## 2.1    Clients and others who contribute to the client function

If you require services from a builder or architect, you know you are a client and expect to be regarded as such. An individual acting as client presents no problem to those he employs to advise or act for him. They can identify him quite naturally as their client.

Large organizations such as commercial groups, banks, local authorities and housing associations are not so fortunate, however. They can adopt the prime role of client and legally exist as such. They can enter into agreements to appoint consultants or agents and pay them for their services, but they cannot take on the functions of client without organizing their staff to do so. Their size and complexity usually defy the comprehension of outsiders to the organization, unless they reveal their management structure and explain their methods of working to some extent.

Frequently, owners of property are not the occupiers or even long-term owners. Ownership of many office blocks and much housing is vested in development companies, insurance companies and similar trustee organizations. Consequently, it is impossible to establish the requirements of the ultimate occupant, who is quite unknown to the designer. Here, in reality, the institution is only part client, financing and promoting the project as an investment but again not able to take on the functions of client without making special arrangements to define the occupancy requirement from the user's point of view. Public authorities providing hospitals, schools, housing and all varieties of community buildings find themselves in this position also.

Obviously a positive response cannot be expected from professional advisors, designers or agencies if there is ambiguity about the client organization. They need to know a great deal about their client and the people acting for him. It is always beneficial, therefore, to examine the form and composition of the client group. This will help establish a clear and reliable means of communication between the client and all the other people involved in briefing.

Some examples of client types and organizations are set out in Figs 2.3, 2.4 and 2.5. Fig 2.3 raises the question, 'Can any individual deal with

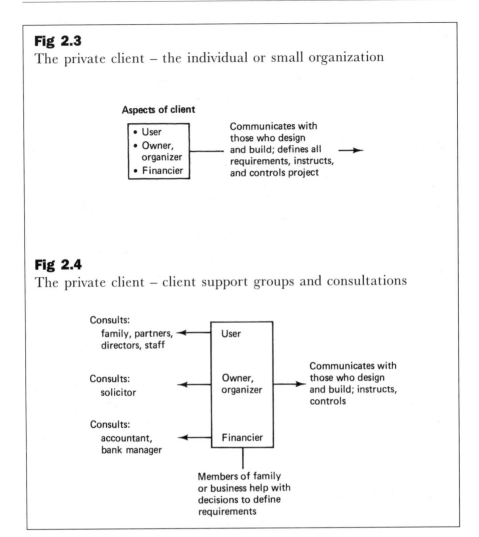

**Fig 2.3**

The private client – the individual or small organization

Aspects of client

- User
- Owner, organizer
- Financier

Communicates with those who design and build; defines all requirements, instructs, and controls project

**Fig 2.4**

The private client – client support groups and consultations

Consults:
  family, partners, directors, staff

User

Consults:
  solicitor

Owner, organizer

Communicates with those who design and build; instructs, controls

Consults:
  accountant, bank manager

Financier

Members of family or business help with decisions to define requirements

all aspects of briefing unaided?' It presupposes a fully knowledgeable and completely supported individual with power to act decisively.

It is more likely that support, guidance and assistance with research is needed, leading to a more developed view of the clients, as shown in Fig 2.4.

Fig 2.3 is how we would like to think we act, particularly as individuals. But Fig 2.4 is much more realistic.

Fig 2.5 displays the elements which make up large and complex client bodies when they are involved in preparing a brief. Each element or group needs to be positively identified and their contributions should be looked for and channelled into the brief. Ideally, the executive group acting for the client needs to handle all the information received and

**Fig 2.5**
The institutional and the public client

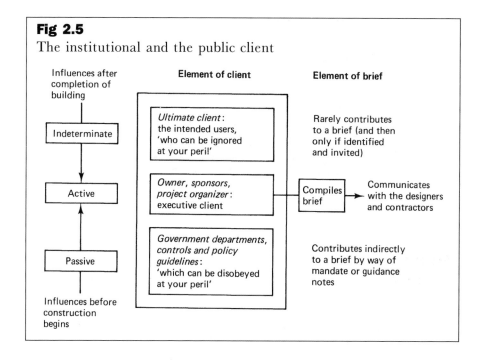

be the only means of communicating it to the designers. However, as all consultants know, the views and wishes of user groups, or the demands or advice offered by a superior organization of some standing, cannot be ignored, but must be attended to by the executive group.

## 2.2 Consultants

### 2.2.1 Those who provide professional services

A number of different professions work in the construction industry. They serve the industry and its clients with specialist knowledge and skill and, in this way, contribute to the design and construction of buildings. Some are highly specialist in the design of interiors or civil or mechanical engineering works.

These professions act as agents or consultants. They will work either as individuals or as part of a team along with other professionals.

It is these people who require a brief to work to. They can then collaborate with the client and act for him to develop his ideas and bring them to fruition.

Professional services available include:
o Architecture.
o Building surveying.

o     Civil engineering.
o     Electrical engineering.
o     Furniture design.
o     Graphic design.
o     Industrial design.
o     Interior design.
o     Landscaping and garden design.
o     Mechanical engineering.
o     Project management.
o     Quantity surveying.
o     Structural engineering.
o     Town planning and urban design.

It is not necessary to engage separate consultants to obtain all these services on every project, although most of the specialisms may be needed to some degree.

In practice, a wide range of expertise is collected within professional practices of differing size, composition and character. By far the largest number of professional firms are small, with one or two principals, a few assistants and other support staff, and they provide a wide range of services, embracing a number of the specialisms set out above. The smaller professional practices providing these services to the industry fall into the following groups:

o     Architects.
o     Quantity surveyors and building surveyors.
o     Engineers of various kinds:
  —   Civil and structural.
  —   Mechanical and electrical.
o     Specialist designers.

Each practice is individual in its composition, styling and experience. Whilst being orientated to one profession, such as architecture, the principals can possess additional qualifications in others, such as town planning, surveying or interior design. Also they may include, as part of their firm, staff qualified in disciplines such as landscape architecture or structural engineering, in order to offer a wider, more comprehensive service.

### 2.2.2  Information about practices – directories

To assist clients in understanding the breadth and type of knowledge and skill of architectural practices, The Royal Institute of British Architects publishes a *Directory of Practices*. It sets out particulars such as:

o     Practice name and address.
o     Names and qualifications of partners.
o     Number of partners.

○    A statement prepared by the practice giving examples of their buildings.
○    An indication of whether the practice is interested in small works, conversions, alterations and one-off houses.

The Royal Institution of Chartered Surveyors publishes similar details about surveying practices in their *Year Book*. It lists under each practice the various aspects of work they undertake. Also, to assist with identifying and selecting engineering practices of all types, the Association of Consulting Engineers publishes a *Consulting Engineers Who's Who and Year Book*.

By contributing to these directories and year books, practitioners assist those searching for particular expertise and experience to find a practitioner or firm that suits them.

These reference books are a source of valuable information for all who know of their existence and understand how to use them. The art is to know where to look and to be a discerning reader!

### 2.2.3  Collaboration and interdisciplinary working

However it might seem, it is rare for one firm to be sufficiently equipped to deal with all aspects of a large project. Clients should expect the practice first approached to recommend that additional specialist help be sought from other practitioners.

In all but the smallest of domestic projects, some collaboration between professions is necessary. Usually two or three professional people need to work closely together so that all specialized requirements of a building are properly researched and designed. For example, when an architect deals with the heating, ventilation or artificial lighting of a building, he quite often needs to call on the expertise and experience of specialist designers. They could be part of his own firm or be independent consultants. Their role would be to implement or interpret the architect's initial designs, or contribute fully in the decisions made at the briefing and early design stage.

Some common groupings of professions and relationships between consultants are set out in Fig 2.6 and the chart on p. 31.

### 2.2.4  Multi-disciplinary practices

Some consultancy and contracting organizations have expanded over the years in an endeavour to provide an all-in service. They group under one roof a wide range of professional expertise.

Examples of firms set up in this way are:
○    An architectural practice offering project management, architectural design, town planning and urban design, and comprehensive

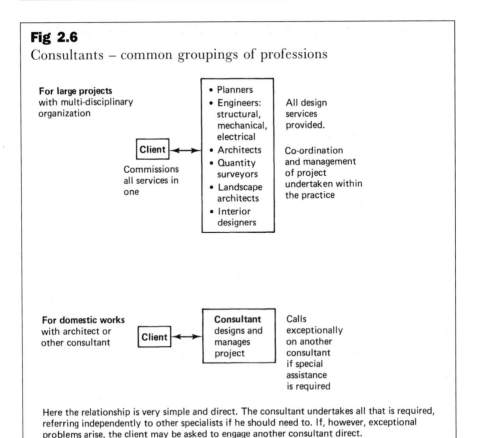

**Fig 2.6**

Consultants – common groupings of professions

**For large projects**
with multi-disciplinary organization

Client

Commissions all services in one

- Planners
- Engineers: structural, mechanical, electrical
- Architects
- Quantity surveyors
- Landscape architects
- Interior designers

All design services provided.

Co-ordination and management of project undertaken within the practice

**For domestic works**
with architect or other consultant

Client

Consultant designs and manages project

Calls exceptionally on another consultant if special assistance is required

Here the relationship is very simple and direct. The consultant undertakes all that is required, referring independently to other specialists if he should need to. If, however, exceptional problems arise, the client may be asked to engage another consultant direct.

design services in interiors, furniture, engineering and industrial design, and also landscaping, graphics and a financial and quantity surveying service.

o    A large contracting firm offering project and financial management services and architectural and engineering design services in addition to their construction knowhow and capability. Their services are comprehensive and fully professional. Often termed package deal, turnkey or design-build contracts.

o    A quantity surveying practice offering building economics advice, help with contracting options, project management and project cost control services, together with a building surveying and refurbishing and building repair design service.

o    A structural engineering practice with a wide range of design and site supervisory services to offer in civil engineering, general engineering and architecture, and also financial, landscaping, project management and interior design services.

---

**Step-by-step approach – client to architect (involving other specialist consultants)**

1. *Client*
   Seeks advice.
   Defines brief.
   Gives instructions.

2. *Architect*
   Receives instructions.
   Researches problems.
   Begins designing.

3. *Architect needs technical and specialized contributions*

   Option A: Consults without reference to client

   | EITHER expertise is part of architect's own practice: | OR architect consults specialist at his own cost: |
   |---|---|
   | works with a structural engineer or quantity surveyor (partner or employee). | obtains opinions, data or design material from town planner. |
   | Costs are either absorbed in fee or specifically agreed with the client at the time the architect is commissioned. | Fee is borne by architect – if more extensive work is needed, the client would be asked to agree appointment (option B). |

   Option B: Asks client to commission consultants separately

   | Project needs cost advice, estimates of costs and bills of quantities: | Project needs structural calculations and designs: |
   |---|---|
   | architect recommends appointment of a quantity surveyor. | architect recommends appointment of a structural engineer. |

   *These appointments are separate contracts between the client and the consultant.*

   However, all communications concerning the project go through the architect, who co-ordinates and manages the project.

o      A local authority architectural department with design expertise in architecture, mechanical and electrical engineering, quantity surveying, interior and industrial design, landscape architecture, site supervision and building surveying. Its services are coordinated within the department.

Highly successful organizations exist which operate in this way. Their achievements and the publicity given to them brings these multidisciplinary practices to the attention of the industry and general public. They demonstrate the value of in-house collaborative working within the common goal of a parent organization. Contrary to general opinion, these firms are not restricted to working exclusively on large, complex projects. They can also bring together a few of their professional staff to deal with quite small commissions.

## 2.3    Contractors

Building contractors are those who organize and carry out the construction activities necessary to produce the building envisaged by the designers. Normally, one organization controls the works. It brings to bear knowledge of accepted building methods and techniques and a special skill in tackling the problems which can arise with each type of site or building.

The services of building contractors involve the bringing together of materials, components, equipment and fittings at a location which can be severely exposed to the elements. With less than ideal working conditions, compared to other industries, they must achieve a high degree of precision in the finished structure, be specially watchful to achieve the highest standards of workmanship, and use only materials of appropriate quality throughout – ensuring that building codes and all conventional techniques of good building practice are maintained. They also organize and control the labour required for the building, whilst meeting all safety and environmental standards affecting the building operatives and the locality.

Bringing together the physical part of a structure is a major undertaking. Even more so is the organizing and planning of the order and timing of each of the contributing trades and their activities, and the hire and positioning of cranes, hoists, scaffolding and temporary plant and equipment. All this requires vision and experience.

Vital as the contractor's expertise is in the construction phase, it is not entirely restricted to this phase. The participation of contractors in the briefing and early design stages of a project is seen as valuable. Steps can be taken to involve contractors well before site construction begins.

## 2.4    Contracting firms

In essence, all builders and contractors give the same services. But they appear to be widely different kinds of organizations. They range from small builders with a few retained tradesmen, to vast nationally spread organizations with branch offices and associated subcontracting firms. In spite of the image each presents, the significant differences are to do with:

o    The type and size of project they undertake.

o    The type of client they seek to serve.

The greater percentage of contracting firms employ less than 10 people doing repairs and maintenance and some minor project works. Although relatively few, the 70 to 80 largest national firms carry out about a quarter of the value of UK contracts. One section of large contractors concentrates on civil engineering work only.

Most contractors will respond to invitations to construct projects to the detailed designs of architects, engineers and designers. Sometimes builders are willing to advise the client directly, and even do the design work (or employ an architect to produce the design drawings). When adaptations or extensions are needed to a small house or office building, quite often a builder is approached first of all and he looks after the whole exercise for the client from beginning to end. In a similar fashion, both the design and construction of large industrial or commercial buildings are undertaken by large contracting firms.

Nearly all project work is done in a fragmented fashion, however. The professional design services are provided by one firm and the contracting services by another. Invariably, this second firm divides up part of the work between a number of subcontractors. The majority of UK contractors maintain a regular workforce of tradesmen. Usually only those working in trades like bricklaying, carpentry and concreting are retained. Other work is let out to independent firms specializing in particular trades, services or installations. Examples are: natural stonework, roof coverings, structural steelwork, piling, precast concrete floors and other products, glazing, plastering, wall tiling, painting and decorating, and the design, supply and fixing of heating, ventilating, electrical and gas installations and manufacture and supply of prefabricated components of all kinds.

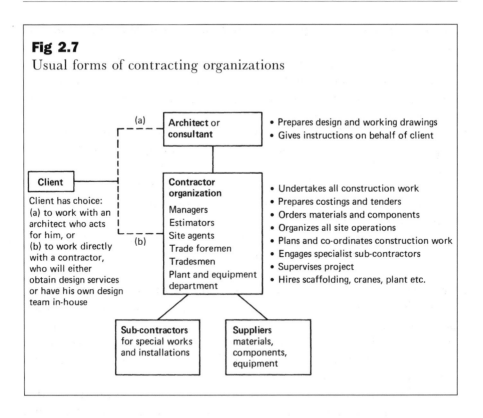

**Fig 2.7**
Usual forms of contracting organizations

With the tendency to specialization growing, the general contractor is nowadays only directly involved in executing about a quarter or a third of the project. However, the managing of all site operations, and the planning, coordination and supervision of the subcontractors, is an important task of some magnitude, the contractors most skilled in this field being the most successful.

Finding a suitable contractor presents an equally confused picture to enquiring clients as does the selection of consultants. Understanding how contracting firms organize themselves is a help, but there is no national scheme for classifying firms. The only directory which exists at present appears at the beginning of *Houses Guide to the Construction Industry* but this is restricted to the contract experience of major firms only.

The usual form of contracting organizations and their relationships is shown in Fig 2.7.

## 2.5 The stage is set – or is it?

Isolating and identifying the three main groups and the forms which they may adopt helps with pinpointing what each participant does –

the part the client, designers and constructors will play in the building enterprise.

Interrelationships between them work better when each knows something about the other. But they do not begin to operate until briefing begins. It is the briefing process which sparks off a response between them.

Before briefing progresses too far, however, consider who else might become keenly interested and bring to bear some influence on the project. You can expect some involvement from:

o      Organizations who see themselves as safeguarding society, environmental values or aesthetic standards, such as civic trusts, or conservation groups.

o      Organizations charged with administering regulations which have been prescribed by law, such as planning authorities, and building inspectorates.

Even though uninvited, there are small groups who will involve themselves in the project, bringing unexpected results to the unwary or misinformed client and designer. So it pays to know of building controls which are enforceable, and be prepared to consult with legislating authorities and amenity groups who might find cause to raise their voices against the project.

These make up a fourth group of people who impinge on any project almost without fail – a group which exists as an ephemeral sphere of influence outside the closed circle of activity of the three main participants.

## 2.6    Legislating and safeguarding organizations

### 2.6.1   Statutory authorities

*e conomical   ddmin*

Government departments and local authorities exercise a wide range of control over building development work. Their powers flow from Acts of Parliament and other statutes which many people have difficulty in understanding. Theirs is the responsibility for interpreting all the intricacies of the legislative documents, and the granting of approvals.

A schedule of the Acts of Parliament and some of the key regulations which affect building work is set out in Figs 2.8 and 2.9. The organizations which sanction development or give approvals under those regulations are indicated on it, and the particular official or department to approach in the first instance.

One way to avoid difficult encounters is to find the correct point of contact. For example, the building regulations include strict requirements

## Finding the correct person to talk to in your local authority office

| Subject matter | Officer and local authority |
|---|---|
| Extensions permitted without approval. Planning submissions and outline proposals. Whether buildings or trees are protected. Policy about development in the locality. Regional development plans. Noise pollution and acceptable standards. Maximum heights of buildings. | *Planning Officer* of District Council or County Council |
| Building regulations: application forms. costs. inspections. submission dates. Safety of buildings and retaining walls. Street lighting. Constructing a vehicular access to a street. Locations, depths and sizes of local authority sewers. | *Chief Technical Officer* or *Building Surveyors* or *Divisional Engineer* to District Council |
| Fire prevention, escape routes from buildings. Methods of fire-resistant construction. | *Chief Fire Prevention Officer* of District Council |
| Advice about: Security of buildings and their contents. Planning to prevent ease of break-in to buildings. Alarm systems. | *Chief Crime Prevention Officer* of District HQ of Metropolitan or County Police Force |
| Surface water disposal. Sewer connections. Blocked sewers. | *Engineer* to either: Regional Water Authority or District Council |
| Height of chimneys. Hygiene in public buildings (kitchens). Housing grants. | *Environmental Health Officer* of District Council |
| Music and dancing licence. Liquor licence. | *Local Magistrates Clerk* at local Magistrates Courts |
| Petrol licence. | *Petroleum Inspector* or *Environmental Health Officer* of District or County Council |

**Fig 2.8**

Building regulation approval – the usual procedure

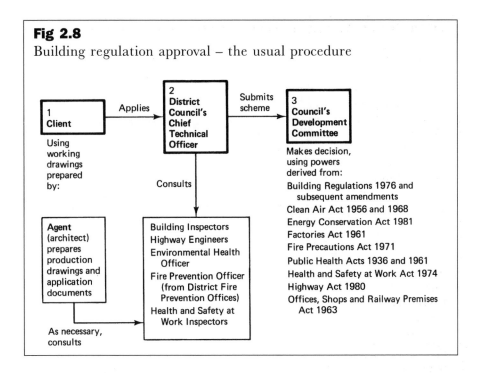

about fire precautions – compartmentation, means of escape, methods of construction and varying degrees of fire resistance for the materials to be used. When detailed working drawings are submitted, well after the designs are complete, meticulous checks are made by the local authority building inspectors. However, their methods include consulting a fire prevention officer from the local Fire Brigade headquarters. To be sure the drawings are approved and the building design survives this hurdle, it makes sense for the architect to consult the fire prevention officer directly at an earlier design stage – well before the scheme design drawings are finished.

Applying the various Acts to particular projects, and the routine and method of obtaining approvals, are intricate and arduous. Experienced consultants know the most successful procedures to use, early informal consultation with responsible key people being a vital one.

Direct approaches to a local authority's chief planning officer to obtain informal comments is an example. It may lead, of course, to his participation in the evolving design. He may have strong views, perhaps preferences for certain architectural forms or colours of materials. Negotiation then becomes unavoidable – an unwelcome step as far as the design team is concerned. But it may be helpful to remember that although a local authority's planning committee is not bound by its

**Fig 2.9**

Planning approval – the usual procedure

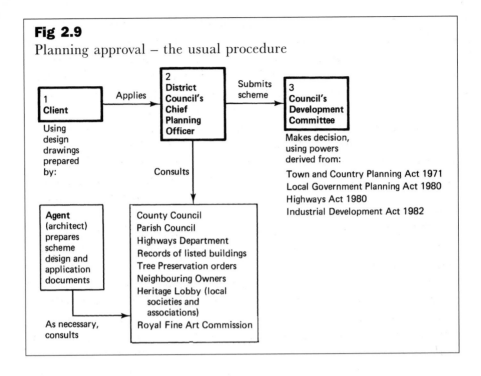

planning officer's opinion, it will in all probability respect his views, so
early consultation is advisable.

This is also true when seeking some reassurance about the obtaining of building regulation approval, or the views of an amenity group.

### 2.6.2  Health and Safety Regulations

Taking care of the health, safety and welfare of people in the workplace is a general concern which has attracted a great deal of new legislation during the last decade or so.

A recent addition in European Community Countries is the *Health and Safety Construction (Design and Management) Regulations 1994* (CDM Regulations) which affect building projects. This European law places new legal obligations on all concerned with the construction and maintenance of buildings: architects, designers, contractors and also *clients*. The Regulations apply throughout the life of the building. This is because the intention is to eliminate unnecessary exposure to foreseeable risks for all persons working on buildings, when constructing and subsequently maintaining or cleaning them. Failure to comply with the CDM Regulations is a matter for criminal proceedings.

Of immediate concern to the client is the requirement to make two key additional appointments: those of Planning Supervisor and Principal Contractor. Here we find the CDM Regulations impose the need to formally engage additional professional services. It is most likely that the client will ask the architect to take on the additional responsibilities of Planning Supervisor and the main contractor those of Principal Contractor – although the Regulations accept that one person can be appointed for both roles, or that a client with appropriate expertise may elect to undertake the duties. Whoever adopts these roles, however, must be fully competent in health and safety matters and it is the client's responsibility to be satisfied about their competence.

The Planning Supervisor is appointed during the early briefing and design stages with the main task of establishing a Health and Safety Plan. This is a document which sets out overall arrangements for the safe operation of the building throughout the years to come after it is completed and brought into use. The Principal Contractor is expected to help develop the Health and Safety Plan before construction works commence and is also responsible for ensuring that safe working methods and practices are used on the construction site.

Because clients in the UK have a duty to comply with the CDM Regulations they should seek advice and guidance particularly when assessing the competence of a professional who is to act as a Planning Supervisor. The Health and Safety Executive offers general guidance and advice and area offices can be approached for help.

Here we find intruding into the project a further set of influential people in the form of the Health and Safety Executive who oversee the implementation of the CDM Regulations and are empowered to enforce them.

### 2.6.3  Amenity groups

The fourth group of people who can become involved in the project can be extended even further. Civic trusts and conservation societies are established in most localities. They undertake a safeguarding function for society. If active and vociferous, they can be quite influential.

In the UK a wide variety of interests are represented, as the names of the following examples show:

The National Playing Fields Association
Council for the Protection of Rural England
Historic Buildings Council
National Monuments Record

Royal Fine Art Commission
The National Trust
Nature Conservancy Council
British Property Federation
Arts Council of Great Britain
The Victorian Society
The Civic Trust

(Most bodies have branches in Scotland, Northern Ireland and Wales, and many have local or regional offices.)

Some development schemes are passed to local civic trusts and conservation groups by planning authorities for comment, and their views are taken into account. Parish councils are also consulted. It is their role to become informed about all important projects in their area, and provide a forum for debate to help define local opinion and the views of the amenity groups.

It may be considered wise not to approach representatives of legislating organizations, or even amenity groups, any sooner than absolutely necessary. To any property developer, or a citizen needing approval for a straightforward extension to his house, the safeguarding function is a hindrance. It may conflict with his wishes and even block his scheme completely. What the layman may not know is that hardly any building development or improvement scheme can be put in hand without first obtaining planning permission. Should an application be rejected, the subsequent procedures for appealing, or the adjusting of the project, are very onerous, costly and time-consuming. By far the best course of action is to consult before placing a formal application. A major development proposal can cost many hundreds of pounds in fees to the planning authority alone, when the application is formally submitted. Loss of valuable time and redesigning and resubmission costs can be avoided if preliminary consultations are undertaken.

## 2.7   Obtaining professional advice and services

How does a client find the professional advice most suited to his project? Is there a method of locating practitioners or consultant organizations?

There are a variety of possible steps which can be taken, but no general procedure which can be recommended. Some options open to the client are set out on p. 41. A combination of some of the suggestions is probably the best course of action.

| | |
|---|---|
| 1. A direct approach to professional institutes, either at their headquarters or regional or branch offices, requesting their client advisory or information services. | Each institute offers prospective clients the names of two or three suitable firms, in response to enquiries stating the nature of the project and its location. General advice about procedures can also be obtained. |
| 2. To respond to publicity, advertisements or circulars sent out by professional firms and contracting organizations. | Practitioners are permitted by their professional bodies to advertise their services in a modest and responsible manner. |
| 3. To seek out and respond to recommendations of people or organizations which have recently had construction work done for them. | Look for completed buildings which are of interest and approach the occupiers, owners or contractors for more information. |
| 4. To search through professional directories of practitioners. | See directories published by the Royal Institute of British Architects; Royal Institute of Chartered Surveyors; Association of Consulting Engineers; and the Architects' Registration Council of the United Kingdom (available in the reference sections of public libraries). |
| 5. To enquire at the local Citizens' Advice Bureau. | A free, comprehensive advisory service provided by local architects is available to anyone who needs guidance. The service operates like a doctor's surgery. Telephone for surgery times. |
| 6. To approach large contracting organizations or management contractors, who may be able to offer an all-in design and construct service. | Most large organizations will advertise their services. Otherwise, refer to practice directories which give an idea of the size and composition of the firm, and any branch offices they may have. |
| 7. To approach large multi-disciplinary professional firms, who may include all or most design, financial and management skills in-house. | |

## 2.8 Selecting a firm or practitioner from a shortlist of choices

When making a final choice between firms or practitioners, particularly those offering architectural services, it is advisable to:

o     Interview the principals, partners or directors.

o     Find out how they are organized.

o     Examine some of their completed buildings.

(Time spent doing this will be time well spent.)

For large, prestige projects the shortlisted firms might be asked to submit a simple short-term feasibility design to present their ideas about the project and indicate their approach to any problems which may be inherent in the site or the client's requirements. (The fees involved will prove to be money well spent.)

It is wise to compare professional organizations or individual architects and give them opportunities to demonstrate their design ideas. However, the exercise is competitive in nature and every firm involved should know what is being done. Any competitive design submitted should not be expected free of charge.

If it is thought better to invite ideas from the architectural profession as a whole, an open competition can be set up with the assistance of the Secretary of the Royal Institute of British Architects.

## 2.9 Commissioning and agreeing fees to be paid

During preliminary discussions with an architect, a point will be reached when an initial idea of the type of building work required

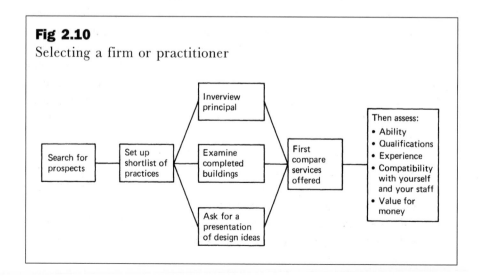

**Fig 2.10**

Selecting a firm or practitioner

becomes clear. Only then can steps be taken to establish the value of the architect's fee. The way it is arrived at is given below.

o    *Agree with the architect the services you require during each of the phases the project has to pass through.* These are called work stages and they are based on the RIBA Plan of Work, which is described in Chapter 3 of this book.

— A schedule of services should be provided by the architect. Those which apply to all commissions, those which are needed during the outline and detail design stages of your project, and those applicable to the services required during the tendering, construction and completion stages.

— A flexible approach to progressing the project might be appropriate. The client might decide initially to limit the commission to particular activities such as preparing designs sufficient for a planning application to be made.

o    *Agree the percentage fee which is applicable to the project.*

— The architect should have already sent the client a copy of a booklet giving guidance about architectural services and fees.

— Professional fees are usually calculated as a percentage of the cost of the building work. The guidance booklet displays in diagram form the percentage figures which apply to different classes of building and shows the percentages graduated over a range of different project costs.

— Using these diagrams, in discussion with the architect, a percentage figure can be arrived at acceptable to both parties, or a lump sum fee.

— Fees are a matter for negotiation and agreement. There is no firm or recommended scale of fees. The diagrams referred to above have been produced by the Royal Institute of British Architects to assist clients in the UK judge what is a reasonable fee. These diagrams have proved to be a good and workable guide. When designing, time and care is needed to explore and develop the client's ideas and requirements and look after his interests. Clients who severely restrict time and money for this purpose, and architects who accept such limitations, proceed at their peril.

o    *Agree the expenses which are to be chargeable.*

— The cost of printing drawings, postage and fax charges, travel costs and overnight accommodation, where relevant, are normally charged by all professions.

— All fees paid to local authorities on behalf of the client, when submitting applications for building regulation or planning approval, to be reimbursed.

○     *Agree fees for any special services which may be required.*

—    If the architect is to act as project manager or planning supervisor or provide special services, such as landscaping design, interior design, the making of measured surveys, or preparing special drawings or models, settle the additional fee which the client is to pay.

When precise architectural services and fees are agreed, appointing the architect can take place. The client commissions the architect to undertake the project and grants authority to the architect to act for him. The final step to take is:

○     *Agree the Conditions of Appointment supplied by the architect.*

—    A document setting out conditions of appointment needs to be agreed by the client when formally commissioning the architect. It is usually a standard printed form used by the architectural profession as a whole. Clauses in the agreement not already discussed with the architect should, of course, be clarified if not understood.

—    This is the last chance to review what each party is taking on as a firm commitment.

## 2.10    Summary

With some background knowledge about how consultants and contractors are organized, and how they relate to one another, the client is better equipped to seek out the professional services which will suit him.

The client will be able to:

○    Decide about the kind of consultant to approach first.

○    Identify more correctly the professional services which will suit him, his organization and the project he has in mind.

○    Probe beyond the professional directories, advertising literature or front person, to discover how the practice or organization is made up and how it operates.

○    Work more confidently with the organization or practitioners selected to build up a brief.

Whatever you, as client, choose to do, you must produce an outline brief, a detailed considered statement of your needs. If you opt out and leave the designers with little information and few leads (whatever organization you choose), you will be faced one day with an uncontrollable situation. You will be offered a welter of sketches, diagrams, reports and costings which you may find hard if not impossible to relate to your needs.

# The brief in its context

This chapter will help you to decide:

o   What the client is expected to do and when he should do it.
o   How much detail to include in your descriptions of what you need.
o   What comes first and what details to leave until later on in the process.

It will also help you to understand the work stages the design goes through and where the brief fits in.

Briefing takes priority in the sequence of activities which leads to the commencement of site works. It is the most important contribution the client can make to the building project. It is as creative as anything the architect or other designers subsequently do. This does not mean that it is a short-term activity to be got out of the way quickly. It should never be rushed or done in a cursory fashion. Even in the smallest of projects, time is needed to refine and develop the brief.

After the outline brief has been produced, the architect has to assimilate its requirements into his initial designs. In addition, the client needs to consider other options. There is a tendency for clients to think of the widest possibilities and include almost unrestricted demands on the building, so some adjustment of first aspirations is usual. Also, as facts about the site and other constraints are collected, more changes to the brief have to be made.

With the brief continually developing as each stage of review and amendment takes place, it takes time before it becomes settled enough for a realistic design to be produced. But does this not cause a delay?

## 3.1    The relationship between briefing and designing

Briefing extends throughout the design stages of a building project. It becomes a parallel activity with those of the architect and other designers. This is normal.

The now well-established plan of work (see *Plan of Work for Design Team Operations*, RIBA Publications, 39 Moreland Street, London EC1V 8BB), which was evolved by the Royal Institute of British Architects in 1973, defines the stages through which all design briefs go when they progress from inception to completion. An extract from the outline plan of work is reproduced in Fig 3.1. During stages A to D the brief grows from a sketchy, tentative outline or first try into a quite detailed statement representing the client's considered and firm ideas about the full extent of his requirements.

## 3.2    Gradually compiling a brief

This method of compiling a brief suggests that every client needs to build it up whilst feasibility studies and user studies are taking place, and whilst initial sketch plans are being prepared. Some may not be convinced that this is appropriate and most productive. A once and for all effort to write a complete brief at the inception may seem more worthwhile. Could not the architect and other members of the design team then work independently, being untroubled by holdups and frustrations created by regular contact with their client?

Highly experienced clients, organizations which build often, can produce a great deal of documentation at the start. At inception stage they can usually hand to the architect the equivalent of a full brief for the building they require. Examples would be a property development company requiring an office building or a local education authority department requiring a new school.

It is unlikely, however, that such a client would dispense with the architect's recommendations about the feasibility of the project, particularly in terms of finance and architectural form. The outcome of feasibility studies and surveys into site conditions, alternative forms, design possibilities and user requirements often influences the client to change the original brief in his best interests.

It is unwise as a general rule to attempt to achieve too much too soon. If standardized documents exist, they are of course very useful. However, in practice they come to be regarded more as a reference brief. The statements and data set out, however successfully used in the past, need systematic review in the light of the project currently

## Fig 3.1
Outline plan of work (copyright RIBA Publications Ltd)

| Stage | Purpose of work and decisions to be reached | Tasks to be done | People directly involved | Usual terminology |
|---|---|---|---|---|
| A. Inception | To prepare general outline of requirements and plan future action. | Set up client organization for briefing. Consider requirements, appoint architect. | All client interests, architect. | Briefing |
| B. Feasibility | To provide the client with an appraisal and recommendation in order that he may determine the form in which the project is to proceed, ensuring that it is feasible, functionally, technically and financially. | Carry out studies of user requirements, site conditions, planning, design, and cost, etc., as necessary to reach decisions. | Clients' representatives, architects, engineers, and QS according to nature of project. | |
| C. Outline proposals | To determine general approach to layout, design and construction in order to obtain authoritative approval of the client on the outline proposals and accompanying report. | Develop the brief further. Carry out studies on user requirements, technical problems, planning, design and costs, as necessary to reach decisions. | All client interests, architects, engineers, QS and specialists as required. | Sketch plans |
| D. Scheme design | To complete the brief and decide on particular proposals, including planning arrangement appearance, constructional method, outline specification, and cost, and to obtain all approvals. | Final development of the brief, full design of the project by architect, preliminary design by engineers, preparation of cost plan and full explanatory report. Submission of proposals for all approvals. | All client interests, architects, engineers, QS and specialists and all statutory and other approving authorities. | |

in hand. What at first looks like a final brief produced at inception stage turns out to be really an outline brief. Although a lengthy and detailed statement, it still fits in at the first of the evolutionary steps which are embodied in the RIBA Plan of Work, and is subject to inevitable modification.

So clients starting afresh – or any inexperienced person having to start from scratch – need not feel particularly disadvantaged. This applies to staff newly transferred or recruited to project briefing for a highly expert client organization, or individuals commissioning building works privately.

The act of creating a first-time brief being of necessity a gradual affair, is really no more demanding than checking through a previously used collection of documents to review, substantiate or alter them. After all, the whole process is to do with obtaining the best possible view and judgement of what is really needed in a building.

When writing a brief for the first time, the client's attempts at setting down the required features and type of accommodation will be vague. When it is realized that these first attempts are a valuable embryonic contribution, there need be no hesitation.

In subsequent stages of work many opportunities arise to test and reconsider the first ideas, and bring any conflicting elements of the outline brief into focus. Aspects of the project which are of strategic importance become clearer. Views of colleagues or potential users come to hand and there is also an interchange of ideas with the designers. As designing begins and tentative forms or alternative arrangements of the proposed building are produced, the incentive is created which encourages both client and designers to work hard to achieve a coincidence of aims. This process is conducive to the production of a full and complete statement of requirements – a final brief.

## 3.3    Completion of the brief before designers are appointed

If a full brief has to be produced before design work begins, it presents some special difficulties. Any client attempting this task independently at the inception of a project requires special skills. Past experience of brief writing and an awareness of architectural possibilities are vital. A good example is the setting up of architectural competitions.

Competition conditions include a brief which is prepared by the sponsors with the assistance of experts: usually an architect and a manager or owner of the building type which is the subject of the competition. Because the sponsors cannot anticipate how individual architects will interpret the brief in built form, many questions are

## Development of the brief: some evolutionary steps

| *Client action* | *Material for brief* | *Consultants' action* |
|---|---|---|
| **RIBA Stage A – Inception** | | |
| ● Considers need to build.<br>● Sets up supporting organization (working party, committee or representative).<br>● Appoints consultants.<br>● Commences exchange with consultants.<br>● Provides information for outline brief. | ● History of events leading to decision to build.<br>● Details of client and consultants firms, personnel.<br>● Time-scale for the project.<br><br>*Outline brief*<br>● Policy decisions.<br>● Purpose and function of project.<br>● Details of site and services.<br>● Basic details of building requirements, and cost limit. | ● Carry out preliminary consultations and appraisals of buildings or sites.<br>● Receive and examine outline brief. |
| **RIBA Stage B – Feasibility** | | |
| ● Conducts user studies.<br>● Considers feasibility results and analytical studies and reports.<br>● Develops brief. | ● Additions/amendments to outline brief in as much detail as possible about: site conditions; space requirements; relationships and activities; interior environment; operational factors.<br>● More precise information about client's financial arrangements. | ● Survey and study site and locality.<br>● Consult statutory authorities.<br>● Conduct feasibility exercises and studies of features of the brief.<br>● Advise about meeting of cost time limits.<br>● Elicit information required, and guide and assist with collection of brief. |
| **RIBA Stage C – Outline proposals** | | |
| ● Receives and appraises designs and reports.<br>● Receives and approves outline designs and costs. | ● Amendments and additions to brief as a result of appraisals.<br>● Completed room data sheets. | ● Produce first sketch designs for analysis.<br>● Complete outline design and cost plan.<br>● Complete informal negotiations with statutory authorities. |
| **RIBA Stage D – Scheme design** | | |
| ● Receives and approves full scheme designs and costs (if satisfactory).<br>● Instructs preparation of presentation drawings.<br>● Authorizes formal submission for required statutory consents. | ● Amendments and more details.<br>● Layouts, etc., of furniture and equipment in special rooms and areas. | ● Prepare full scheme designs and estimate of costs.<br>● If approved, prepare presentation drawings, perspective sketches and/or models.<br>● Apply for planning and other consents. |

At this stage correlation between the brief and scheme designs should be complete – each interprets the other.

posed by competitors. To be fair to all, answers given must be compatible with the way the sponsors originally envisaged the project. There is then little scope for developing the brief to embody changes which could lead to a more workable or imaginative architectural solution.

To many architects the competition system is seen as a means for selecting an architect. Glamorous and exciting perhaps, but a selection process nevertheless. Winning designs are rarely realized in their entirety when built.

Promoters frequently sanction radical adjustments to the interior arrangement or general form before construction takes place. Possibly, they learn from a study of other notable designs submitted and the assessor's views about them. Also, design changes will occur naturally from the sponsor's relationship with the successful architect. Whatever the character of the relationship, whether friction exists or not, the original competition conditions will be questioned and reviewed as though they were an initial brief. So it is a natural step to revert somewhat to the normal briefing process to test the conditions and reconsider the architectural design.

The experiences of competition promoters demonstrate some key points about the place the brief assumes in relationship to the design process. These are:

○     *The brief should not be used as the sole means of communication between client and architect*. It is less effective for client and designers to work in isolation.

○     *Gradually build up the brief in stages with the participation of the architect*. Designers more easily absorb the client's wishes and weigh the problems they set up when they are revealed progressively, as the brief develops. Strategic points in the brief are then less likely to be omitted from their designs.

---

### Architectural competition

There are broadly three types of competition:

1. Competition for an actual building, conducted in one or two stages.
2. Competition of ideas arranged to elucidate particular planning problems or sensitive architectural points.
3. Developer/architect competitions.

All are valid methods for promoting architectural projects or comprehensive central area development schemes. For more details, would-be promoters should consult the Secretary of the Royal Institute of British Architects and obtain a copy of their *Regulations for the promotion and conduct of competitions*.

o      *Involve the architect at the time the brief is reviewed, extended or amended.* Clients benefit more when they know the designer's reactions to the brief. They learn more of the consequences of the constraints inherent in it as the design takes shape on the drawing-board.

o      *Use the brief to collect the views of users before designs progress too far.* User reaction and some user involvement is possible when designs are being produced. Negative responses to completed designs can then be avoided or reduced.

## 3.4    Relationship of the brief to the remaining work stages

When the brief is finished, when it reaches as complete a state as possible, it stands as a record of all the client's requirements. But its life and usefulness are not over. During the period when working drawings and specifications are drawn up, the designers will continue to refer to it, if it is informative and precise.

Clients may not realize how much reliance is placed on their brief. Time spent thinking out and compiling the more detailed parts, like room schedules and descriptions and dimensions of fittings, is amply repaid. It can help greatly with correctly specifying and locating items such as:

o      Sanitary fittings.
o      Handrails.
o      Power outlets.
o      Wall finishes.
o      Floor finishes.
o      Window sills.
o      Door widths.
o      Door furniture.
o      Lighting levels.
o      Special fittings, etc.

In fact, its usefulness extends well into the construction stage when site works are nearly finished. It can aid during pre-handover checks to establish whether all items detailed in the brief have been supplied and correctly positioned.

A brief is, therefore, not limited to aiding the production of an architectural design. Its purpose is very much extended to describing the building in its final state of completion. It exists as a mainstream of influence and instruction from the client to all engaged in bringing the project to fruition.

There are occasions when a brief is not fully completed at scheme design stage. Under certain circumstances the briefing process can extend into the working drawing and tendering stages. Final details concerning the interior arrangement and furnishings can be left undecided if it is not necessary to know the precise costs of the work as the contractors begin site works. By including provisional amounts of money – or 'provisional sums' – in the building contract, it is possible to defer decisions about items such as:

o	Moveable partition units, lighting fittings, office equipment, kitchen fittings and isolated features such as railings, barriers and gates, or special floor finishes.

o	Sunblinds, curtains, artwork, interior landscaping and loose furniture – especially those items not affecting the building structure and service installation pipe runs.

o	The design and location of notices, signs and door nameplates, until immediately prior to completion of construction works.

o	The final positioning of specialized fittings and built-in furniture until the client can see the effect of his decisions *in situ* – this could happen in kitchens and when disabled persons are to use the building.

This method is quite usual and practical, but adopting it still involves the client in making broad decisions about the type and extent of the items of work whilst the brief and scheme designs are being completed. All that is deferred, therefore, is the detailed decision making and design work.

However, whilst being a convenient and perfectly valid method to follow, there are serious disadvantages which a client must face. The process encourages late changes of mind which can lead to disturbance of completed work when the contractor is striving to complete the building. Late completion and an increase in construction costs then becomes inevitable, and a great deal of friction can arise as a result.

*If intending to extend the normal period of briefing beyond scheme design stage*, take particular care to:

o	Leave undone only those items which can cause least harm when the building is being constructed.

o	Discuss with your consultants any proposals to defer work, and only put them into effect if they can assure you that no harm will come of it.

o	Observe conventional methods, such as including provisional sums equal to the intended cost of the late installations in the agreed contract sum.

o	Not delay too long making decisions about the outstanding items of work. They are really forming a second-stage brief which must still be completed in time to fit into the designer's and contractor's work timetable.

One occasion when briefing extends beyond the scheme design stage is when a contractor is asked to begin building work before the working drawings are complete. Some projects are timetabled in this way in order to secure an early physical start, after a schedule of costs for measurable units of the construction works is agreed.

If involved in this kind of contract, a client would endeavour to complete enough of his brief to be able to approve the scheme design drawings before allowing a start to be made on the site. The second stage of the brief would then be compiled and worked on with the architect as a matter of urgency. Otherwise a great many decisions would remain to be taken by the client almost up to the completion of the project.

## 3.5    Development of the brief

Fig 3.2 displays the normal method of building up a brief through the various work stages of a building project (work stages are as defined by the RIBA Plan of Work).

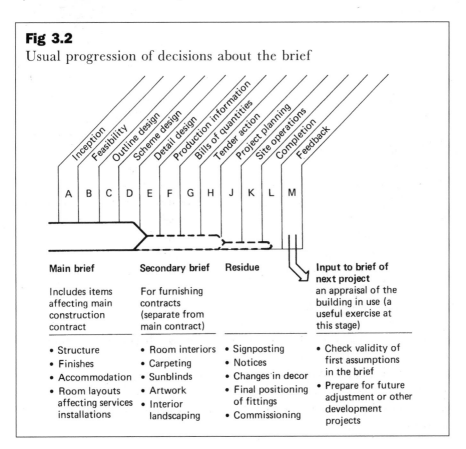

**Fig 3.2**
Usual progression of decisions about the brief

| Main brief | Secondary brief | Residue | Input to brief of next project |
|---|---|---|---|
| Includes items affecting main construction contract | For furnishing contracts (separate from main contract) | | an appraisal of the building in use (a useful exercise at this stage) |
| • Structure<br>• Finishes<br>• Accommodation<br>• Room layouts affecting services installations | • Room interiors<br>• Carpeting<br>• Sunblinds<br>• Artwork<br>• Interior landscaping | • Signposting<br>• Notices<br>• Changes in decor<br>• Final positioning of fittings<br>• Commissioning | • Check validity of first assumptions in the brief<br>• Prepare for future adjustment or other development projects |

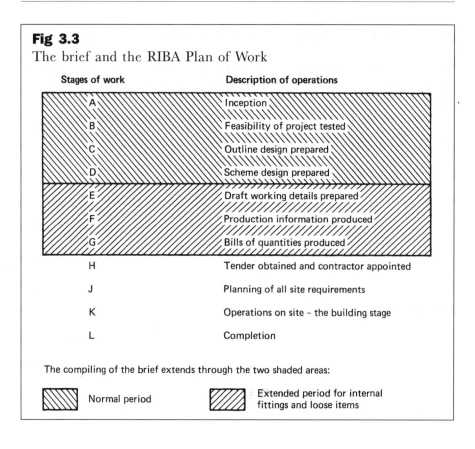

**Fig 3.3**
The brief and the RIBA Plan of Work

| Stages of work | Description of operations |
|---|---|
| A | Inception |
| B | Feasibility of project tested |
| C | Outline design prepared |
| D | Scheme design prepared |
| E | Draft working details prepared |
| F | Production information produced |
| G | Bills of quantities produced |
| H | Tender obtained and contractor appointed |
| J | Planning of all site requirements |
| K | Operations on site – the building stage |
| L | Completion |

The compiling of the brief extends through the two shaded areas:

Normal period

Extended period for internal fittings and loose items

An extra source of information for a brief is shown in stage M in Fig 3.2. If a study is made of the performance of a building after six or nine months of occupation, it will help a client to:

o    Check the correctness of the provisions and assumptions included in the original brief.

o    Review the decisions which helped to shape it.

o    Bring to light critical factors affecting the use or management of the building which may have not been fully appreciated before.

The value of this kind of appraisal is, first, that it provides the client with tested material for inclusion in the brief of another building, if he has similar buildings to construct in the future; and, second, that it provides invaluable material for consideration when the building is altered or extended should this be needed in the future, to contribute to the brief which would be needed at that time.

Of course, first-time clients would not have feedback of this sort to draw on. But there is always an opportunity to look at the way other people's new buildings perform in practice.

## 3.6    The RIBA Plan of Work – how to make use of it

The RIBA Plan of Work was introduced by the Royal Institute of British Architects to assist design teams when working together on large, complex projects. It is an acknowledged procedural guide for the construction industry in the UK. It is relevant and useful when compiling a brief and can be used in the following ways.

### 3.6.1    Method 1

○    Keep before you the outline of work stages and relate to it the work you are doing.

○    Decide on the nature of the immediate task in hand and decide where it fits into the stages of work.

○    Determine its relative importance in the chain of activities to be carried out.

○    Then, knowing the purpose, context and relative importance of a task, you can decide how much detail to go into and how decisive to be. (Sometimes people will produce highly detailed descriptions at the inception stage [stage A], or take an inordinate length of time to reach a decision about an item which will inevitably be affected by later sequences of building up the brief or refining the designs.)

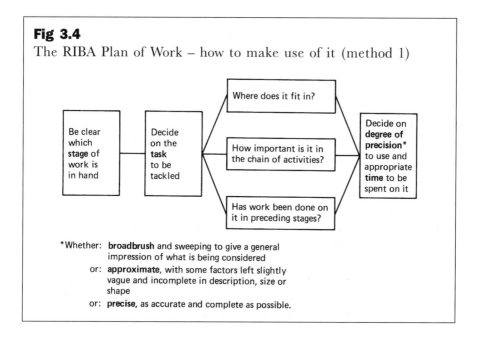

**Fig 3.4**
The RIBA Plan of Work – how to make use of it (method 1)

Be clear which **stage of work** is in hand → Decide on the **task** to be tackled

Where does it fit in?

How important is it in the chain of activities?

Has work been done on it in preceding stages?

Decide on **degree of precision\*** to use and appropriate **time** to be spent on it

\*Whether: **broadbrush** and sweeping to give a general impression of what is being considered

or: **approximate**, with some factors left slightly vague and incomplete in description, size or shape

or: **precise**, as accurate and complete as possible.

### 3.6.2   Method 2

Another method is to use the detailed charts in the RIBA Plan of Work as a guide pointing to the steps to take through each of the stages (see Fig 3.5). When referring to 'Plan of Work diagram 4 stage C', for example, each column can be regarded sequentially, defining the essential activities of client, architect, quantity surveyor, engineer and contractor, and portraying the order and priority of their work (see Fig 3.6). Clients as well as consultants benefit from a study of these diagrams. They provide opportunities for considering and planning:

○     How one fits into the activities which are described and the part one should play in them.

○     The tasks other people are to do and what to expect from them.

○     The collaborative nature of the work and how to be sure full collaboration takes place.

○     Whether tasks are properly completed and whether all consultants are kept abreast of all changes and developments.

○     Anticipating and preparing for each succeeding step before it happens.

Newcomers to the industry should not think of the RIBA Plan of Work as a pattern which is to be followed slavishly. It is better to regard it as a framework of activities in which one identifies the relationship of the work in hand to other stages in the design and construction of a project. Trying it out in this way will prove that the client and consultants are able to communicate more effectively and understand better what each is doing.

**Fig 3.5**

The RIBA Plan of Work – how to make use of it (method 2)

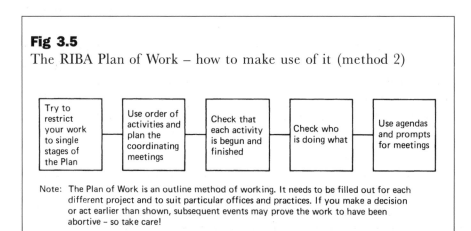

| Try to restrict your work to single stages of the Plan | Use order of activities and plan the coordinating meetings | Check that each activity is begun and finished | Check who is doing what | Use agendas and prompts for meetings |

Note:   The Plan of Work is an outline method of working. It needs to be filled out for each different project and to suit particular offices and practices. If you make a decision or act earlier than shown, subsequent events may prove the work to have been abortive – so take care!

There is no doubt that participants in building projects progress through RIBA Plan of Work stages even if they are unaware of it. Experience shows, however, that each project develops in a different way. The design team may find they need to backtrack to earlier stages of work, to recasting of designs or redrafting the brief, schedules and specifications. But this in no way invalidates its usefulness.

The Royal Institute of British Architects says that 'The Plan of Work is essentially a work planning and coordinating tool that must be adapted to the particular circumstances and must never become a "strait-jacket" imposing inappropriate procedures.' For full details of the RIBA Plan of Work refer to *Plan of Work for Design Team Operations*, available from RIBA Publications, 39 Moreland Street, London EC1V 8BB.

### 3.6.3 Example of the usefulness of the RIBA Plan of Work when quoting estimates of cost during the development of a project

A highly important aspect of a project is its likely cost. When building works are first thought of, the cost of professional fees and the overall construction cost are of concern. The client needs to budget and organize financial support for his project, and the consultant is pressed early on for a rough estimate.

In order to satisfy the client, assumptions have to be made. There are two sides of the equation: the extent of the proposed works and the cost. Not even an informed guess is possible without sure knowledge of the site, its location and the quality of the project. Consultants dislike quoting their ideas of the cost until they can be based on agreed designs or a firm brief. They fear that clients will fasten on the figure stated and expect the cost never to be exceeded, despite the inevitable changes the project undergoes during the design stages. Additionally, the circumstances surrounding the consultant's attempt to forecast the project cost are usually forgotten.

Misunderstandings can be avoided if the RIBA Plan of Work stages are referred to when quoting estimated costs. The figure quoted can be placed firmly in the context of the conditions prevailing at the time it is produced, and the degree of accuracy of the figure can then be related to the stage reached in the development of the project. An example showing how this might be done is given below.

---

**Order of cost at stage A, inception stage**

£150 000 including fees, based on initial brief for extensions of 1000 square metres and visual inspection of site in City Road.

---

## Fig 3.6

RIBA Plan of Work stage C (outline proposals) (copyright RIBA Publications Ltd)

## Stage C   Outline proposals

Plan of work diagram 4

To determine general approach to layout, design and construction, in order to obtain authoritative approval of the client on the outline proposals and accompanying report.

| Col. 1<br>**Client Function** | Col. 2<br>**Architect**<br><br>**Management Function** | Col. 3<br>**Architect**<br><br>**Design Function** | Col. 4<br>**Quantity Surveyor Function** |
|---|---|---|---|
| 1. Contribute to meeting: note items on agenda in Col. 8. | 1. Organise design team. Call meeting to discuss directive prepared in stage B, action 9 (Col. 2): establish responsibilities, prepare plan of work and timetable for stage C. See Col. 8 for items for agenda for meeting. | 1. Contribute to meeting: note items on agenda in Col. 8. | 1. Contribute to meeting: note items on agenda in Col. 8. |
| 2. Provide all further information required by architect. Assist as required in all studies carried out by members of design team. Initiate and conclude according to timetable, any studies that are required within own organisations.<br><br>Make decisions on all matters submitted for decision relevant to stage C. | 2. Elicit all information relevant to stage C by questionnaire, discussion, visits, observations, user studies, etc. Initiate studies by consultants and client as required.<br><br>Maintain and co-ordinate progress throughout this stage. | 2. Carry out studies relevant to stage C, e.g.:<br><br>(a) study published analyses of similar projects, visit if possible.<br><br>(b) study circulation and space association problems.<br><br>(c) try out detail planning solutions and study effect of planning and other controls. | 2. Carry out studies relevant to stage C, e.g.:<br><br>(a) obtain all significant details of client's requirements relevant to cost and contract information on site problems, etc.<br><br>(b) re-examine, supplement and confirm cost information assembled in stage B. |
| | | 3. In consultation with team assimilate information obtained in action 2, and produce diagrammatic analyses, discuss problems. | 3. Outline design implications of cost range or cost limit. |
| | | 4. Try out various general solutions; discuss with team; modify as necessary, and decide on one general approach. Prepare outline scheme, indicating, e.g. critical dimensions, main space locations and uses and pass to team. | 4. Collaborate in preparation of outline scheme. Prepare quick cost studies of alternative structural and services solutions, and advise on economic aspects of solutions. |
| | | 5. Assist QS in preparation of outline cost plan; discuss and decide on cost ranges for main elements, and method of presentation of estimate to client. | 5. Confirm cost limit or give firm estimate based upon user requirements and outline designs and proposals. Prepare outline cost plan in consultation with team, either from comparison of requirements with analytical costs of previous projects or from approximate quantities based on assumed specification. |
| | 6. Compile dossiers provided by team members on final (or alternative) sketch designs, recording all assumptions, and issue to all members of the team. | 6. Contribute to design dossiers, assemble all sketches and note relevant assumptions. | 6. Record basis of estimate to contribute to design dossiers. |
| | 7. Prepare report as co-ordinated version of all members' reports, including fully developed brief. | 7. Contribute to preparation of report. | 7. Contribute to preparation of report. |
| 8. Receive architect's report; consider, discuss and decide outstanding issues. Give instructions for further action. | 8. Present report to client; discuss and obtain decisions and further instructions. | | |

| Col. 5<br>**Engineer**<br>**Civil and Structural**<br>**Functions** | Col. 6<br>**Engineer**<br>**Mechanical and Electrical**<br>**Functions** | Col. 7<br>**Contractor (if appointed)**<br>**Function** | Col. 8<br>**Remarks** |
|---|---|---|---|
| 1. Contribute to meeting: note items on agenda in Col. 8. | 1. Contribute to meeting: note items on agenda in Col. 8. | 1. Contribute to meeting: note items on agenda in Col. 8. | **Items for agenda for meeting:**<br>1. *State objectives and provide information:*<br>(a) *brief as far as developed*<br>(b) *site plans and other site data.* |
| 2. Carry out studies relevant to stage C, e.g.:<br>(a) site surveys, soil investigation.<br>(b) complete questionnaires on structural and civil requirements. | 2. Carry out initial studies relevant to stage C, e.g.:<br>(a) environmental conditions, user and services requirements, appraise M & E loadings on an area or cube basis.<br>(b) consider possible types of installation and analyse capital and running costs, possible sizes and effects of major services installations, main services supply requirements. | 2. Carry out studies relevant to stage C, e.g. visit site and investigate:<br>(a) ground conditions, access and availability of services for construction.<br>(b) local labour situation.<br>(c) local sub-contractors and suppliers to assess quality reliability, production potential and price level, etc. | (c) *re-state cost limits or cost range, based on client's brief.*<br>(d) *timetable.*<br>(e) *agree dimensional method.*<br>2. *Determine priorities.*<br>3. *Define roles and responsibilities of team members and methods of communication and reporting.* |
| 3. Advise architect on, e.g.:<br>(a) types of structure.<br>(b) methods of building.<br>(c) types of foundation.<br>(d) roads, drainage, water supply, etc. | 3. Advise architect on design implications of studies made e.g.<br>(a) factors which would influence efficiency, and cost of engineering elements, i.e. site utilization, building aspect and grouping, optimum construction parameters, etc.<br>(b) possible services solutions and ramifications of them.<br>(c) regulations and views of statutory authorities. | 3. Advise architect on findings and also on:<br>(a) approximate times for construction of alternative methods.<br>(b) effect of construction times on cost, etc. | 4. *Define method of work, tender procedure and contract arrangements.*<br>5. *Agree drawing techniques.*<br>6. *Agree systems of cost and engineering checks on design.*<br>7. *Agree type of bill of quantities.*<br>8. *Agree check list of actions to be taken.*<br>9. *Agree programming and progressing techniques.* |
| 4. Collaborate in preparation of outline scheme, prepare notes and sketches, consider alternatives, agree decision on general approach, and record details of alternative plans and assumptions. | 4. Collaborate in preparation of outline scheme, check that services decisions remain valid; record details of alternative plans and assumptions. | 4. Collaborate in preparation of outline scheme: continue to advise on time and cost implications of alternative designs or methods. Record details of proposals and assumptions. | |
| 5. Provide QS with information for outline cost plan, with sketches on which to base estimate, and agree QS proposals. | 5. Provide QS with cost range information for outline cost plan, and agree QS proposals: interpret agreed standards by illustration. | 5. Provide QS with information affecting price levels, for outline cost plan and agree QS proposals. | |
| 6. Compile dossier of essential data collected in actions 2 to 5 above. | 6. Compile dossier of essential data collected in actions 2 to 5 above. | 6. Compile dossier of basic cost information agreed with QS and architect. | |
| 7. Contribute to preparation of report. | 7. Contribute to preparation of report. | 7. Contribute to preparation of report. | The report includes:<br>(a) the brief as far as it has been developed;<br>(b) an explanation of the major design decisions; and<br>(c) firm estimate with outline cost plan. |

An illustration of how an estimate of cost would be expressed at different stages of work is given here:

## Blankwich Day Centre

| | | | |
|---|---|---|---|
| *Stage A* | Order of cost of £150 000 (excluding professional fees). | Based on | • Initial brief.<br>• Schedule of rooms.<br>• Floor area of 1050 square metres.<br>• Visit to site and knowledge of coal-mining subsidence problems. |
| *Stage B* | Preliminary estimate: £178 000 (excluding professional fees). | Based on | • Brief (as at 1 March 1986).<br>• Floor area of 1175 square metres.<br>• Survey of site.<br>• Mineral valuers' and engineers' reports.<br>• Room relationship diagrams 7, 8 and 9. |
| *Stage C* | Updated estimate: £176 000 (excluding professional fees). | Based on | • Brief (as at 25 April 1986).<br>• Floor area of 1127 square metres.<br>• Full site and subsoil investigation.<br>• Sketch plans 15,16 and 17.<br>• Preliminary cost plan. |
| *Stage D* | Approximate estimate of cost: £181 000 (excluding professional fees). | Based on | • Brief (as at 17 July 1986).<br>• Floor area of 1098 square metres.<br>• Full site and subsoil investigation. |

|  |  |  | • Structural engineer's initial designs.<br>• Scheme design drawings 26–32.<br>• Full cost plan and outline specification. |
| --- | --- | --- | --- |
| *Stage F* | Cost check (final): £183 750 (excluding professional fees). | Based on | • Working drawings.<br>• Engineering design.<br>• Full specification.<br>• Amended cost plan. |
| *Stage G* | Forecast of tenders: £180 050 (excluding professional fees). | Based on | • Bills of quantities (priced by quantity surveyor). |
| *Stage H* | Lowest tender: £168 784 | Included in tender submitted by Messrs XYZ Construction Co. (checked by quantity surveyor). | |

# Creating a healthy working relationship

o     How to clear away any uncertainties and suspicion and build confidence.

o     How to conduct the first meeting with your architect.

o     Finding out how to build up mutual understanding.

o     Gaining an understanding of how to contribute to the first meetings with the architect and consultants.

If the client, his architect or any of the design team members find that they are not in tune with each other, there is a danger of the briefing process going sadly wrong, resulting in an unsuccessful building and an unhappy experience for all concerned. Professional standing and ability will, of course, be the first thing a client thinks of when choosing his consultants, but the creation of a sympathetic working relationship is also very important.

Understanding and mutual trust are essential to a sound relationship where everyone pulls together to try out ideas and solve problems. But this does not always come about naturally.

On p. 64 is a typical case of a client and an architect meeting for the first time and getting off on the wrong foot owing to their preconceived impressions. Each has opinions cultivated from past experiences or the views of other people.

There is a lot here which could be resolved if both client and architect talked frankly about their uncertainties and how each intends to operate.

At their first meeting, time should be devoted to getting to understand each other, clearing away uncertainties and suspicions, and creating a cordial atmosphere where each can have confidence in the other. This also applies when meeting the rest of the design team for the first time.

| Client as seen by architect | Architect as seen by client |
| --- | --- |
| • He could be indecisive and change his mind often. | • He could confuse me with technicalities. |
| • He could dictate the appearance and form of the building. | • He might use a type of construction or architectural style I do not really want. |
| • He might want a very early start on site and curtail my design time unreasonably. | • He might pay far too much attention to the appearance of my building, and leave me with technical faults to correct. |
| • He might not understand how much work I have to do and consider my fees too high. | • He might cause delays which make a mess of my cash flow prediction. |

If this is not possible, it is better by far to terminate the relationship without delay. Better a courteous letter at this stage, suggesting that 'I did not feel we were right for each other, and thank you for the courtesy of allowing me to talk to you,' than a continuing relationship which leads to increasing unhappiness, discord, a faulty brief and an unsuccessful building project.

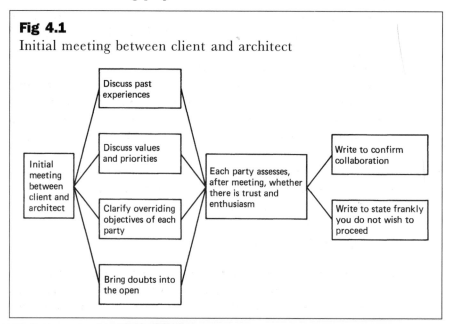

**Fig 4.1**
Initial meeting between client and architect

## 4.1    Initial steps

### 4.1.1   For all clients

o  *Find out what the consultant is able to do for you.*
o  *Ask him what he expects you to do as client.*
o  *Take the architect or project manager into your confidence.*
>      When first meeting, there should be a frank discussion about
>      the professional services to be given and the client's part in
>      building up the brief.
o  *Discuss architectural style and construction techniques to determine the
architect's general approach to your project.*
o  *Satisfy yourself about his objectives and philosophy.*
o  *Use the architect and designers as sounding boards for the ideas you have.*
>      It is too soon to be precise about the appearance of the build-
>      ing, but the subject of architectural style should not be shelved.
o  *Set a firm, feasible programme.*
o  *Be clear about how much you want to spend.*
>      There are some matters the client cannot be vague about,
>      such as his objectives and financial limits.
o  *Find out what your responsibilities are as client.*
>      The consultants must be open and clear about their fees and
>      the length of design time they anticipate needing. See also
>      Chapter 5.
o  *Have a single, clear liaison route.*
>      One person in the client's firm or family should communicate
>      with one person in the consultant's firm. This is the ideal
>      arrangement, whatever the project is.
o  *Agree how to continue with briefing and design.*
>      Both parties must be approachable and have enough time
>      available to give priority to communicating with each other.
>      Do not expect rapid progress from an architect unless you can
>      respond quickly to all questions he raises. Be prepared to meet
>      often.

In this way, you help to remove any tendency to be suspicious, feel
uncertain and act indecisively. You begin a process which fosters mutual
understanding between client and consultant.

### 4.1.2   For large client organizations

The following are in addition to the steps set out for all clients.
o  *Select the staff who will be associated with building projects on your behalf.*
>      Qualities and skills which would be looked for when selecting

staff are set out in a specimen job description on p. 71. Staff should have the status and ability to operate confidently with minimum direction and supervision.

○ *Educate staff who are to liaise with consultants and manage their activities and ensure they are adequately informed about briefing methods.*

There are no courses available or formal training methods. Individuals chosen to act as briefing or liaison officers would have to do private research of available publications. Instruction could be given by your consultant or an experienced liaison officer from another client organization.

○ *Instruct liaison staff fully about your organization.*

○ *Ensure they know who to approach for decisions.*

○ *Be sure they have the authority to seek out information required by the consultants.*

Induction courses are necessary for new members of staff. Special authority and instructions may be needed from the policy group or board of management.

○ *However big your organization, appoint one liaison officer with full authority to act as your representative.*

○ *Give the liaison officer authority to call on any department or manager for immediate assistance.*

○ *Avoid changing liaison staff too often and retain key personnel if possible.* The consultants should have only one person to refer to. When they do, they are more likely to get prompt and positive results: information and decisions which are authoritative and supported by your organization. Do not assign this person to another post during the briefing and design stages of a project.

○ *Try to free liaison staff from other duties during the time a brief is being compiled.*

Staff with other work to do for your organization cannot be expected to set it aside to liaise with consultants and manage your organization's decision making and fact finding. A good client does not cause delays when designs are being prepared because he cannot find time to respond to questions – or just cannot organize his staff to do so.

### 4.1.3 For architects

○ *Find out what arrangements the client intends to make to carry out his part of the briefing.*

○ *Ascertain whether he is conversant with the professional services which are available and knows which disciplines are needed to satisfactorily tackle his project.*

Experienced clients will need little help to organize for briefing. Nothing should be taken for granted, however. Always tell a client what you expect of him.

○    *Inform the client and any liaison staff about the part they are expected to play when briefing.*

○    *Take the client along with you as the brief and design take shape. Inform him frequently as they evolve. Maintain regular contact.*

The education of a client and his staff can only be done gradually. For a first-time client of a large building, it is worth devoting much time to this.

○    *Learn all you can about the client's attitudes to the industry and professional services.*

○    *Find out if he has preconceived ideas about how the building should look or the form it should take.*

○    *Discuss how unwise it is to allow preconceptions to take the place of an open attitude to the natural development of the design.*

Obtain the client's comments and note his expectations. This could alert you to correct mistaken ideas about the need for a full study and systematic approach to the evolution of a design. Consider setting up a presentation.

○    *Explain how you intend to tackle the project.*

○    *Describe any special or exploratory planning or design exercises you intend to undertake.*

○    *Describe the composition and structure of your practice and the professional qualifications of the partners and staff.*

By being quite open about your intentions and attitude to the project, and about the internal workings and nature of your practice, you are making a positive move to reassure the client and build up his confidence in you. Without such action, he cannot be expected to respond.

○    *Assign a partner, or job architect, as liaison person on behalf of your practice.*

A single route for all communications via one of your architects is vital to building up a reliable means of communication. Discourage contacts with other members of staff.

At the first meetings, opportunities will arise to open up mistaken attitudes or preconceived ideas, for the purpose of reaching a mutual understanding.

To disregard anything a client might be ignorant or misinformed about, and press on with the project, hoping the designs will be approved, can leave an underlying threat to harmonious working relations. Should a lack of coincidence between the aspirations of a

**Fig 4.2**
First working meetings between client and architect

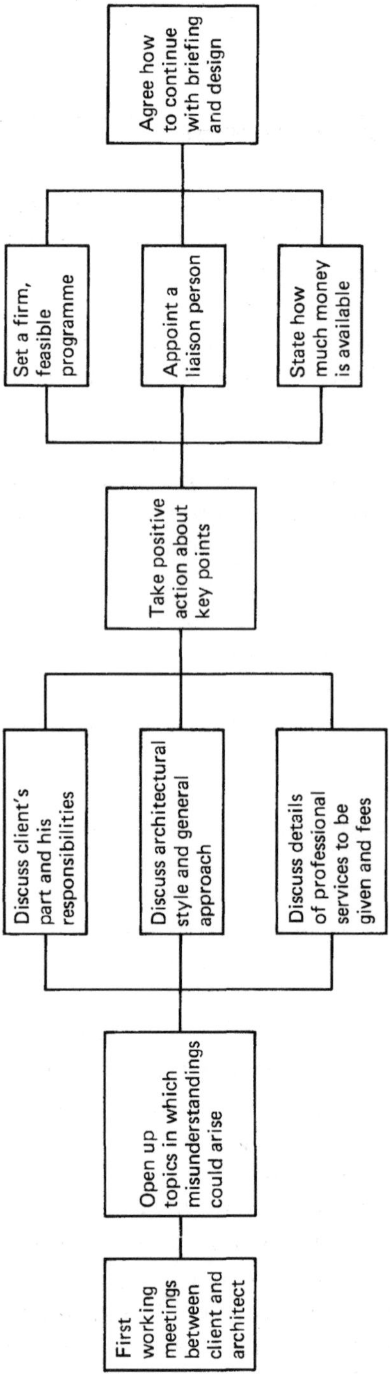

client and the vision of an architect arise in this way, then the client is bound to become suspicious and uncertain about the architect and his services.

## 4.2 After the preliminary meetings

When concluding the first meetings, the participants could feel a glow of satisfaction because their initial objectives are fulfilled: a project started for the client and another fascinating job for the architect. At this time both parties should:

o     Take stock of the position reached at the first meetings.

o     Ascertain whether a sound relationship can be established or whether inadequacies were observed.

o     Find out if uncertainty is apparent or a lack of awareness about the complementary role each plays in the relationship.

o     Look for signs from the other, such as those given below.

*Client of architect*

Is he: genuinely sympathetic to my objectives?

taking up my requirements quickly and fully?

easy to understand?

ready to allocate enough qualified people to my project?

*Architect of client*

Is he: aware of the intricacies of starting up and seeing a project through?

naive or experienced?

prepared to follow through the envisaged building when problems arise, as they surely will?

Both parties should take a cold look at the new relationship, particularly if two large organizations have set up representative teams to undertake the preparatory meetings. Ask whether the other party or team seems to be:

o     Open-minded and willing to listen?

o     Decisive, imaginative and trusting?

o     Well organized with a clear liaison route?

o     Well informed about their role and responsibilities?

o     Offering a flexible, broad approach to briefing and design?

o     Displaying signs of ignorance or suspicion?

An evaluation should be attempted, however difficult it is to assess the attitudes, aptitudes and feelings of other people.

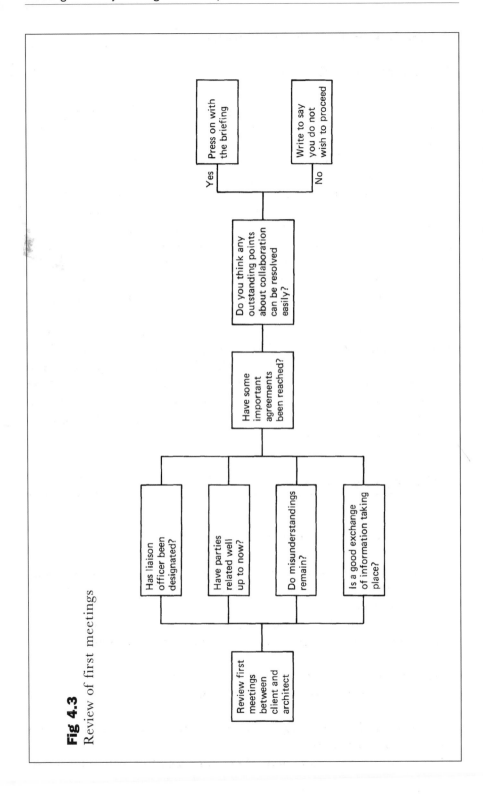

**Fig 4.3**
Review of first meetings

## 4.3     Attributes of those involved in briefing

### 4.3.1    The client's briefing officer

For large organizations acting as clients, the role of briefing or liaison officer is a key one. He needs to be a person of the right calibre, knowledgeable about the special nature of the organization, with the capacity to coordinate, adjudicate and communicate. Key features of the job are given in the specimen job description below.

A large part of his duties are to do with extracting and divining the requirements of his organization. Because he represents the client organization, he must absorb what other people think they need in a building, and understand the relationships of staff and their working methods. He is involved in defining, consolidating and coordinating all the ideas offered and must express them in a form which is truly representative of the organization. In the eyes of the architect, or consultant, the briefing officer is the client.

Fulfilling this job demands much more than desk work or setting up meetings or taking notes. Researching and establishing vital facts involves visiting buildings and libraries, contacting all parts of the client organization, and getting out to meet the consultants working on the project. A special challenge is trying to define the needs of the users and the special needs of the client organization which do not come immediately to mind.

## Briefing officer – job description

*Purpose*
o     Acts as the client's representative and takes executive action from inception to completion of a project.
o     Briefs architects or other professional consultants on the client organization's requirements of new buildings and extensions or alterations to existing buildings.
o     Assists with the formulation of policy matters affecting the quality and type of the organization's building accommodation.

*Nature of operations and responsibilities to be undertaken*
1. Receives outline instructions from managing director or chief officer.
2. Perceives in detail the organization's policy requirements, aims and objectives for verification.
3. Consults with managers and other colleagues to clarify intentions.

4. Collects and develops organization's statement of intent and philosophy.

5. Researches user's viewpoint and investigates specialist or technical requirements and any problems which arise.

6. Organizes and chairs briefing meetings (if required).

7. Presents project to management team and colleagues as it develops, for consideration.

8. Answers all queries raised by architects, engineers and designers, or ensures that the management resolves matters in conflict.

9. Evaluates buildings in use to define user's needs, or any inadequacies, problems or pressure points.

10. Compiles and updates brief.

11. Checks and approves architectural drawings and consults manager and colleagues to ensure that the drawings meet the intentions of the brief.

12. Oversees the commissioning and handover of buildings on behalf of the client.

13. Develops criteria for selection of sites.

*Outline specification of desirable education, qualifications and experience*

A. Essential requirements are:

o    A good general education to cope with the large quantity of reading necessary to keep up to date and prepare well-written statements of intent, leading on to full briefs.

o    A good level of maturity, experience and skill to motivate and extract the best contributions from colleagues and staff at all levels in the organization.

o    Ability to read plans and explain them to colleagues.

o    A first-hand knowledge of the organization's services and operations.

o    Some knowledge of the different facets of the industry, service or profession within which the client organization operates.

B. Special attributes which are an advantage are:

o    An ability to assess priorities correctly and use initiative to keep the liaison activities alive.

o    An artistic ability, particularly to visualize forms and volumes.

o    A stable, equable disposition and an ability to persistently follow systematic methods a little better than most.

o    An imaginative approach to doing the job and stimulating colleagues, users and consultants to think deeply and offer up information and ideas.

### 4.3.2   The individual client – his task and essential attitude

If large organizations need a briefing officer to act for them, what prospect is there for the individual commissioning works for his home, workshop or office block? Perusal of the job description for a briefing officer suggests that an individual client, acting alone, faces a multitude of tasks, probably more than he has the capacity to think about or the time to deal with.

Fortunately the individual client has not got the problems which create the need for a briefing officer. He is able to state his requirements as he sees them and can think and act spontaneously when talking to his architect.

However, there is a discipline to observe which guards against the dangers inherent in a spontaneous and free relationship when briefing an architect. The client should:

o   Note down ideas as they come to mind.

o   Be prepared to talk to other people who expect to occupy the building and take account of their views – it is foolish to ignore them.

o   If there are a number of employees to consult, delegate one to collect the views and suggestions of the others.

o   Take the time to check that the architect understands his requirements.

o   Follow closely the suggestions in this book about how to compile a brief.

# What each party is responsible for

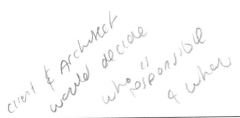

*client & Architect would decide who responsible & when*

**Finding out who is responsible for what and how to discharge your responsibility as client correctly**

A joint approach to responsibility results from:

o  Understanding the position of each party taking part in your project and what they actually do.

o  Understanding the different responsibilities of clients, architects and specialist consultants.

o  Realizing that sensible creative work will not progress far if everyone is concerned about his legal position and the liabilities of others.

Responsibility is a topic which neither consultant nor client would think to bring up at their first meetings. The priorities of starting off the project predominate.

At the beginning of a relationship it is a matter which should not be passed over and 'left until later' – until arguments or problems arise. Knowing who is responsible for what is a key factor affecting the way a consultant and his client work together.

For example, the client has authority and status, and when the extent of his responsibility is clear to the architect and consultants, they know when to look to him for instructions or approvals and when to use initiative. Again, when the roles and responsibilities of the architect and consultants are clear, the client knows what to expect of them.

Being quite clear about the nature and extent of their respective responsibilities when briefing takes place helps to ensure they do not act or commit themselves beyond the point where they can truly fulfil their obligations. It also helps to smooth the working relationship.

Each participant should check that they:

○ Understand the roles each person is undertaking.

○ Know what their essential tasks are and what can be delegated.

Seasoned professionals and experienced clients will, of course, be thoroughly conversant with their responsibilities and know how to discharge their obligations correctly. But those new to briefing, particularly new members of client or consultant teams, should make sure that they understand their position.

## 5.1 The client's responsibilities and essential tasks

### 5.1.1 Identifying a need

○ *Identify the need for a building project.*
  — Initiate the proposal.
  — Make the final decision to build or lease property for alteration.
○ *Select and instruct professional advisers for preliminary studies.*
  — Determine the advice needed.
  — Select consultants or appoint an agent to investigate all aspects of the proposal.
  — Instruct them to conduct surveys and feasibility studies.

It is not too early at this stage to begin working out what accommodation is required and how the building might be constructed. But this cannot be done realistically without obtaining professional advice. (See Section 1.5.2.)

### 5.1.2 Commissioning

○ *Set up design team.*
  — Appoint agent: architect *or* project manager *or* 'package deal' contractor.
  — Appoint supporting team of consultants, including a planning supervisor (as required).
○ *Determine and agree the responsibility of each consultant and formally commission them.*
  — Draw up agreements.
  — Agree fee scales and other charges, such as expenses, and any special services to be given.

Conditions of engagement and recommended fee scales are set out in publications obtainable from all professional institutes (see Section 1.5.3).

o     *Appoint planning supervisor*
  — Appoint architect or other competent professional.
  — Prepare separate appointing document.
A Form of Appointment as planning supervisor and guidance for clients is available from the Royal Institute of British Architects. This appointment is entirely separate from other agreements entered into to provide architectural or other professional services and a separate fee will apply.

### 5.1.3  Providing the brief

o     *Provide an initial brief to state objectives, policies, operational concepts and space needs, including all known facts about the property or site.*
  — Provide statement of requirements.
  — Supply all relevant information about ownership, easements, covenants, consents, record plans, previous surveys and reports.
  — Include historical data.
The client's role in setting up an effective initial brief is crucial to the success of the project. The architect relies on the lead he receives from the client. With reliable supporting data, his task is established.

o     *Communicate requirements in an effective fashion without interruption or undue delay.*
  — Amplify the initial brief.
  — Help the architect to expand or refine the statement of requirements.

o     *Give decisions on all sketch proposals, reports and recommendations, and approve drawings when finalized.*
  — Ensure that the architect understands the data and ideas presented.
  — Evaluate the proposals presented and respond.
  — Ensure that colleagues in the client organization take part in evaluation and decision making.
When evaluating and testing the ideas and proposals put forward by the architect, check if they exceed or fall short of those envisaged initially, and relate to the expenditure limits set.

o     *Compile final brief (or commission architect to do so).*
  — Prepare a full brief for the architect, *OR*
  — Obtain full brief from the architect.

o     *Approve final brief.*
  — Agree contents as representing what the client is asking for.
Some sketch plans will be completed at this stage and will help with testing the brief.

The client's first responsibility is the brief itself. He must ensure that the final brief is fit for its purpose and that it adequately represents his instructions. This overriding function should never be lost sight of.

Acceptance of the brief when finalized signifies that this document represents in law the client's formal instructions. Responsibility for the brief rests with no one else.

### 5.1.4   Delegating part of the client's tasks

It is open to the client to delegate to his architect the compiling of the final brief. The architect would collect together the information and instructions received from the client during the briefing stage and produce a record or final brief. However, the result should be carefully examined to be sure it coincides with the client's wishes.

A busy, preoccupied client might be tempted to engage someone else to complete the brief. But it is not always wise or expedient. Really the client cannot do better than be involved himself. Continual contact with the developing design gives him a keener awareness of the effects of his decisions. He is more able to weigh his priorities and give quicker, more informed, responses.

### 5.2   The architect's responsibilities

The following also applies to any other professional consultant or agency acting as project manager, designer or adviser.

### 5.2.1   Initial advice

o       *Give initial broad advice.*
  —    Give advice or undertake feasibility exercises to help the client appreciate the nature of his site or building.
  —    Assess problems or possibilities inherent in the project or site.
When offering advice and making recommendations, the architect or agent holds himself out as being an expert, fully capable and reliable in every way.
o       *Provide reliable scale plans and technical reports on sites and buildings.*
  —    Undertake physical survey and research.
  —    Consult and report.
The 'as existing' drawings of a site or building are deemed to be accurate, complete and factual. The architect is responsible for ensuring that they are, and that they are fit for their purpose.
o       *Advise about other consultants needed.*

— Suggest type of specialist assistance needed.
— Describe the manner in which they will contribute to the project.
— Indicate conditions of engagement, fees and terms.

The practitioner first approached, whether architect, quantity surveyor or engineer, should acquaint the client with details of the full design services the project requires. Each consultant should endeavour to remove any uncertainties about the nature of the services he is to give. He should state clearly how he and his staff would tackle the project, and not quote estimates of cost or suggest design solutions that ultimately cannot be achieved.

### 5.2.2 Accepting the commission

o   *Receive and accept the commission.*
— Provide a form of agreement for signature recording the extent of the services to be given and the extent of the fees and other charges to be made.
o   *Clarify position as agent for the client.*
— Describe the actions he can take on behalf of the client and obtain authority so to act, committing the client to payment for orders placed and instructions given.

The act of acceptance is more than an acknowledgement of a client's request to act for him. Handing over a booklet setting down general fee scales is not enough. The Royal Institute of British Architects recommends use of the Institute's own points of agreement and insists that its members agree the precise conditions of engagement with a client.

o   *Act for the client and in his interests only.*
— When conducting negotiations, contributing to the brief and designing, strive for the client's objectives and advise him objectively.

The architect lines himself up with the client and works with the client's interests uppermost when designing or giving advice.

o   *Check that the client is commissioning other consultants and agreeing conditions of engagement with them.*
— Obtain copies of draft agreements and clarify the responsibilities of each contributing consultant or specialist adviser.

Unless expressly requested not to, the architect will manage and coordinate the design contributions of other professional consultants. His responsibility usually extends to the effective performance of the total building, and because of this he needs to be able to control the integration of all technical contributions.

o   Inform the client of his duties under the CDM Regulations and make sure he knows that guidance is available from the Health and Safety Executive.

### 5.2.3 Involvement in briefing

○ *Receive the brief.*
— Absorb all facts given and all instructions, ideas and suggestions offered during briefing.
○ *Elucidate stated requirements and elicit all aspects of the brief.*
— Question client to obtain some background to the instructions received.
— Test various alternatives and suggest further studies to be undertaken.
— Request instructions about subjects or items not included in the initial brief.
— Produce diagrams, costings and sketches to elicit responses and promote close consideration of alternatives.

Architects expect to investigate as fully as possible the stated needs of the client. They see it as their responsibility to understand all the influential factors and reasoning behind the instructions they receive. They often wish to learn more about the client's business activities, including a lot of background which might seem irrelevant. It might be considered arrogant to search deeply for influences or hidden aspects of the brief as though the client is not capable of doing so, but this is the architect's way of building up his awareness of his client's design problems.

○ *Record all additions and alterations to the brief.*
○ *If required, collect together a record of the final brief for acceptance by the client.*
— Note down all information, facts and decisions as they arise.
— Amend working records as necessary.
— Produce a final brief reference document (if requested by the client).

If the client's requirements are to stand in a form which can be referred to whilst designing continues, this routine task must be done. It requires great care and diligence. If not collected together in an organized fashion, no final brief exists.

### 5.2.4 Designing

○ *Produce outline designs for approval by the client.*
— Analyse and translate the brief, using diagrams and sketches.
— Analyse and interpret the features and potential of the site (or existing building) using survey data, record plans, analysis diagrams, photographs and sketches.
— Research and assemble relevant facts and general information about the project in hand.

— Explore possible solutions and balance out conflicting influences and demands until a preferred design is evolved and agreed by the client.

The design ideas which evolve, as the meaning and the contents of the brief become clearer, are portrayed in various ways. Rough sketches, diagrams, drawings and computer images assist the architect and the rest of the design team, including the client, to visualize the project, and attract comment, elaborations and suggestions for improvement. When form is given to the ideas presented in the brief, cost planning and estimating become more realistic.

○     *Produce scheme design drawings for approval by the client.*

— Prepare drawings to adequately illustrate the scheme design in its setting and allow its presentation to others.

— Prepare perspective drawings or an architectural model or a full-scale mock-up of a room interior (if the client requests it).

— Produce outline specification of materials and descriptive notes about the design with approximate estimate of cost.

At this time it is possible to see in drawn or three-dimensional form the spatial arrangement and external appearance of the project. Spatial features and some interiors will be illustrated, and a representation of the final colour and texture of materials will be included. Descriptive notes will extend to actual areas and dimensions embodied in the design and the types and qualities of constructional materials and surface finishes.

○     *Obtain the client's instructions to proceed with working drawings and full project documentation in preparation for a building contract.*

— Ensure that the client is satisfied with the scheme design and estimate of cost.

— Check there are no obstacles to obtaining all necessary consents.

— Obtain written instructions to proceed and finally agree method of tendering and contracting, and the timetable of operations through to completion and handover.

This is a fundamental step. Once the scheme design is approved by the client, it represents the client's full intentions. From then on, the architect is responsible for implementing these designs in built form. No radical changes would be made without the client's knowledge and agreement.

### 5.2.5   Overall responsibilities

The full range of responsibilities and duties of an architect are as follows:

○     *Must know the law applicable to all services given.*

— He should be fully conversant with building law, planning legislation and building contract law.

However, it is for the client to obtain his own legal advice about matters which exceed the knowledge that consultants can be expected to have. Architects cannot venture to take on the role of lawyers or barristers.

○ *Must exercise a duty of care to his client and to society in general.*

— This extends to all cases where failure in that duty would cause damage.

— He must in all circumstances act in a fashion in which prudent, experienced fellow professionals would act.

○ *Must exercise a high degree of skill.*

— His special role as a professional implies that he is fully knowledgeable and competent.

— He must check all vital aspects of his work to ensure that they meet currently accepted standards.

Knowledge of the foregoing will explain why so many architects go to such painstaking lengths when obtaining their client's instructions – elaborating and defining the brief, and closely studying the site and all conceivable points about it. Their concern embraces responsibilities which range from those for which they are legally accountable to those for which they are morally answerable.

○ *Has a moral responsibility for the architecture produced and its effect on the environment.*

— He should not disregard the effect a new building will have in a neighbourhood.

In almost any setting, new building creates an impact of some sort. If it is considered as a visual affront or a physical nuisance, emotive reactions can be directed at the client as well as the architect. When this happens, it points to either a wide divergence between the public understanding of architecture as an art form and the architect's own understanding, or an insensitive architect with a disregard for what has been described as good manners in architecture. Either way, it does not leave the client unaffected, and it behoves any client to open up this matter of architectural expression when briefing first begins.

## 5.3  A joint approach to responsibility

The responsibilities of individuals have been highlighted here, but they do not operate in isolation. It will be found in practice that the client can rarely opt out, relying on the architect's reputation – or his indemnity insurance – to see him safely through. The enterprise is strictly a joint one, requiring both parties to be alive to their respective responsibilities.

An architect fulfilling his duties when acting as a brief taker needs corresponding action by the client to fulfil his own duty to provide a brief. Each responds to the other's need. Suppose a client withheld information or failed to expand some points of the brief; it would be open to the architect to refuse to be accountable for any consequences of his lack of knowledge.

Procedures stem from this collaborative approach which should be jointly observed. Examples are:

o    Sufficient time should be allocated to each work stage when producing a brief and design drawings. Both parties need adequate time to make their contributions.

o    An adequate investigation should be made into all user requirements.

o    Contingency plans should be agreed to meet all problems which are suspected but cannot be defined.

### 5.3.1  The need for contingency plans

If problems are suspected – whoever foresees them – joint action is needed. When the client is acquainted with problems, he becomes jointly involved. The risks are evaluated by the consultants and a contingency plan is agreed by the client – perhaps alternative constructional means are devised, or some phasing of the project, or a contingency financial provision is injected into the scheme estimates. In this way each party acknowledges that a risk exists, and together they work out a course of action acceptable to them both.

Some problems which would normally need to be treated as contingency matters are given here as examples:

o    Unknown ground conditions concerning the substrata, groundwater or depth of ponds.

o    Unascertainable information about services, site boundaries or the structural condition of a concealed party wall which cannot be inspected until site works commence.

o    An unpredictable state of the market when tenders are due to be obtained.

o    The expense and delay which could arise from late changes to the brief.

### 5.3.2  A word of warning

The client should always take care not to press his ideas if they are at variance with the advice of his consultants.

If, in spite of advice to the contrary, he pursues a proposal which could affect the safety of property or people, he assumes the liabilities which his consultants would normally carry.

When technical, legal or financial advice is given, the client should always ensure that it is thoroughly understood and that all queries are resolved. He should:

o    Accede to the professional advice offered and support the course of action by granting the necessary authority to proceed; *or*

o    Positively reject the advice and issue alternative instructions.

## 5.4    The legal position

To elucidate the underlying legal position in a book of this kind is not practical. The law is a subject in itself. Court rulings can often alter a point of law which may have stood for years. It is for this reason that the law should always be interpreted by lawyers and barristers.

In the preceding sections the question of responsibility and duty has been presented as a priority matter governing the action of all concerned. Sensible and imaginative creative and construction works will not progress far if everyone has a keen eye on the legal position. However, all qualified professional people will be well instructed and experienced in this subject. Their sense of sound advice and correct action will always stem from a thorough grounding in building law and the legal position of all participants involved in building. It will never be overlooked!

### 5.4.1    The client's position in law

The client, as owner and commissioner of the building, is held to be legally accountable for all contraventions of the law, and anything proved to be detrimental to his neighbours, the public and their property as defined by the law. Whether the client is an individual or an established organization with its own legal identity, this will apply. It concerns both the design and construction phases and the time which elapses affer the building is occupied and brought into use.

However, in meeting any claims for damages, or if facing prosecution, the client may be able to pass on liability to the architect, a specialist consultant, a clerk of works supervising the works, or any contractor or subcontractor employed on the project. It depends on the nature of the problem which has arisen and how clearly the client defined the responsibility of the various consultants and contractors when they were engaged.

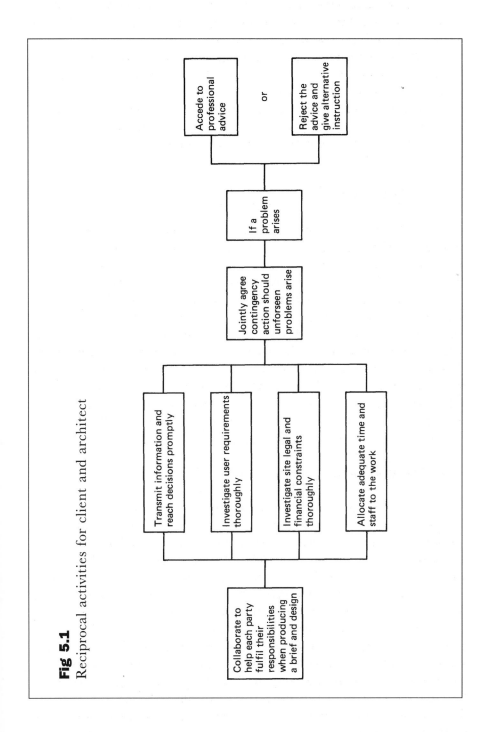

**Fig 5.1**
Reciprocal activities for client and architect

The legal environment in which the client operates can be indicated here, but only in outline and in a very general fashion. What follows can serve as a pointer to suggest various subjects which might be investigated in more depth with the assistance of legally qualified people.

o     *Obtaining sanctions to build.* Town and Country Planning Acts, Highways Acts, Building Regulations, Shops and Offices Act, Petroleum Licence, etc. (see Chapter 2).

— All applications are made in the client's name but completed by the architect or project manager when acting as agent to the client.

— A client would rely on the architect to advise about when and how to obtain all necessary approvals.

— Remember that fees are payable to some sanctioning authorities, and the client is automatically liable for these costs, not the architect.

o     *Respecting the rights of adjoining owners and members of the public.* Common law, London Building Acts, Rights of Light, Tree Preservation Orders.

— The requirements of the London Building Acts do not apply outside London, but they are a good guide about how to proceed when building works affect an adjoining owner in some way, e.g. affecting a party wall, shared services or drains, changing or creating an easement or right of way.

— A client would rely on his consultants' advice about when and how to undertake all necessary negotiations and when to have legal agreements drawn up and executed, but he is ultimately responsible and should, therefore, oversee this work carefully.

o     *Recompensing for injury to persons or damage to property belonging to other people.* Common law, statutory powers of Electricity, Gas and Water Undertakings.

— Insurances covering most eventualities are included in standard forms of contract prepared for the engagement of building contractors.

— The form of contract signed by client and contractor nominates the extent to which the contractor is responsible and the type of insurance which should be taken out on behalf of the client.

— A client relies almost entirely upon the advice of the architect and quantity surveyor about which form of contract to use and which insurances to include in the terms of the contract, but, again, the client is ultimately responsible.

o     *Accepting the responsibility to remunerate the architect and other consultants for the work undertaken on his behalf.* Common law.

— Articles of agreement drawn up between the client and his consultants will specify the fees and expenses which are to be paid by the client and the times when they fall due.

— Whilst not mandatory in law, guidance documents issued by the professional institutes form a good basis for agreements between the client and consultants, indicating a fair level of remuneration for specified stages and types of work.

o  *Accepting responsibility for setting up a strategy for observing the health and safety of all involved in the construction and subsequent maintenance of the building.* Health and Safety Construction (Design and Management) Regulations, statutory powers of Health and Safety Executive.

— Appoints a planning supervisor and a principal contractor and assesses whether both are competent in health and safety matters and that each will allocate adequate resources to comply with the requirements of the Heath and Safety Plan.

— Makes available to the planning supervisor all relevant information concerning the site or the condition of an existing building and also the client organization's safety policies covering the operational use of the building.

— Does not sanction a start on construction work until the principal contractor has developed the Health and Safety Plan.

— Safely deposits the Health and Safety File when received from the planning supervisor on completion of the project.

Appointing a planning supervisor enables the requirements of the CDM Regulations to be set in motion. At that time the client should check that the person or firm selected has the necessary knowledge, ability and understanding appropriate to the project to be undertaken. Subsequently a principal contractor must be appointed, but the client can obtain the assistance of the planning supervisor in making this choice.

However, it is a particular responsibility for the client to be reasonably satisfied when making these appointments that both are competent and have the resources available to readily accomplish the demands made upon them by the CDM Regulations. The client should, therefore, enquire about the level of expertise the designer and contractor can bring to the project and the amount of time their staff are allocated for the health and safety aspects of the work.

### 5.4.2 The architect's position in law

An architect acts as manager, designer and agent to the client when undertaking his role on a project. When carrying out his duties, he must:

o  Know the law applicable to all the services he gives.

o    Exercise a duty of care specifically to his client and also to the public at large.

o    Exercise a high degree of skill.

There is much intricate and detailed legislation which an architect must know about when undertaking project work, much more than can be simply set out here. It is his responsibility to know the law, operate within it and advise his client accordingly. Having a duty of care for his client further emphasizes his need to be conversant with the law and the various procedures involved in all legislative demands on his client.

There are certain key points of law which operate when an architect accepts a commission. He must conduct all his affairs in accordance with their requirements. An architect must ensure he is:

o    *Qualified and registered as an architect to practice in the United Kingdom.* Architect's Registration Act.

—    It is against the law in the UK for a person to adopt the term 'architect' and pass himself off as one when offering services to the public. The Architects' Registration Council of the United Kingdom keeps a register of architects which is published and available for reference.

—    Persons who work as professionals in other disciplines also need to be qualified and their names should appear in the register compiled by their professional institute.

o    *Interpreting and administering the building contract impartially.* The contract after it is signed and sealed applies under the law. Its requirements will be supported by the Courts.

—    When named as architect in a building contract signed by a client and contractor, he must act strictly in accordance with the requirements of the contract when fulfilling its demands and when acting as a quasi-arbitrator.

—    Other disciplines or professions, when named as supervising officer, are bound in the same way.

o    *Acting in a competent manner and checking his actions carefully.* Common law, Articles of Agreement drawn up and signed by the client and architect.

—    When accepting a commission, an architect presents himself as being fully qualified, skilled and experienced, and able to act competently and within all aspects of the law. If proved negligent, he carries the full consequences and costs of rectifying any mistake, or recompensing the client for any loss arising from his negligence or misjudgement. It is for this reason that members of the architectural profession now protect themselves by taking out an indemnity insurance.

— It should be noted that negligence cannot be proved unless it is found that the architect acted in divergence with the understanding and level of practice normal to the majority of practising architects.

## 5.5    Specialist consultants

When other consultants work on a project, they free the architect from some of his responsibilities. Specialist consultants take over responsibility for the contributions they make to the project.

The responsibilities peculiar to each of the major specialist consultants are given below. They are those which apply when the architect is working directly for the client and acts as his agent – managing and coordinating the various contributions as a team leader.

### 5.5.1   The structural engineer

o    *Advises about broad engineering matters affecting the site, foundations and building structure.*
— Becomes involved in those parts of the project for which he has the appropriate technical knowledge and experience.
— Conducts technical surveys and feasibility studies, as requested.
o    *Evaluates structural alternatives.*
— Recommends structurally sound solutions to problems encountered with the building or site.
It pays to engage a structural engineer at the preliminary stage when briefing begins and alternative sites or buildings are being examined. To have detailed engineering advice brings an extra dimension of realism to this stage of the project.
o    *Helps define his responsibilities to the client and architect.*
— Confirms with the architect which elements of the site and building he will work on.
— States any limitations to his responsibility.
— Agrees to act as consultant to the architect, *or*
— Agrees to be responsible direct to the client whilst cooperating with the architect and acting under his direction as team leader.
As the initial designs firm up and the constructional techniques to be employed become clearer, it is possible to define the elements which the structural engineer should work on. This is the time to decide who does what, and draw up agreements with the client or architect.
o    *Probes and elucidates the structural implications of elements of the brief and initial designs.*

— Receives and analyses the brief and architectural design drawings and provides a structural engineering response throughout the design phase.

○ *Interprets and applies engineering standards, regulations and codes of practice in direct support of his own work.*

— Applies up-to-date regulations and codes of practice to the project. Engaging a structural engineer does more than insure against major structural faults. With detailed knowledge of the characteristics of materials and constructional techniques, and a continuing need to refer to legislation about them, he can help with the choice of workable and acceptable structural methods from the outset. This reduces overall design time. Also, delays which could arise from any non-compliance with building regulations are eliminated.

○ *Supplies full structural designs and particulars for combining with the architect's drawings.*

— Collaborates throughout the design stages, supplying designs and advice in drawn or descriptive form to the architect and all specialist contractors and manufacturers.

○ *Supplies detail designs for fabrication and construction of specialist structural elements.*

— At the working drawing stage he produces detailed drawings, specification clauses and critical dimensions of structural elements which become integrated, first into the set of working drawings, and then into the building itself.

A structural engineer is responsible for the advice he gives and the structural adequacy of his designs and specifications, but cannot be held accountable if the architect has curtailed or modified his work.

Because so much structural engineering work is imperceptible in the finished building, his special contribution should never be lost sight of or undervalued.

## 5.5.2   The quantity surveyor

○ *Advises broadly about financial matters concerning the project and development of the site.*

○ *Prepares costings of alternative schemes.*

— Resolves building designs and design ideas into quantifiable units which can be costed.

— Measures and values the materials, component parts, construction processes and labour involved in projects.

— Estimates costs of projects and elements of projects at various times during the development of designs.

— Forecasts future price trends.

— Advises on the cost implications of proposed changes in the brief, or changes in the size, shape and quality of the building.

It pays to engage a quantity surveyor when briefing begins and alternative approaches to the project are being considered. To have detailed financial advice and comparative estimates of cost right from the beginning helps to contain objectives within a realistic financial ceiling. It avoids embarking on flights of fancy and pursuing ideas which are quite unattainable within the available budget.

○ *Prepares financial statements, approximate estimates and cost analyses which serve each stage of a project.*

— Calculates a project cost limit from the outline brief and first design sketches.
— Prepares a cost plan and compares it with cost analyses of similar schemes.
— Produces a preliminary cost estimate.
— Revises the cost plan as the design develops.
— Reviews preliminary cost estimate.
— Prepares a cost check of the scheme design before the client accepts it.
— Produces bills of quantities from measurements taken off working drawings and forecasts the final value of the project: the contract amount.

A quantity surveyor is responsible for correct measurement and estimating of costs, but is not accountable for discrepancies which arise from vague or inaccurate information passed to him. He will work within accepted tolerances of perhaps 5% or 10%. The main value of his work is in guiding the architect and design team towards formulating a design which equates to the finance available. The client should always heed his advice whilst the brief is being evolved and weigh it against the advice offered by the architect and engineers.

○ *Advises about the most appropriate tender procedure to follow.*

— Presents a range of possibilities for consideration by client and architect:
1. *Open competition* – inviting tenders by public advertisement addressed to all.
2. *Selective competition* – inviting only firms that have been carefully selected.
3. *Negotiated tender* – production drawings and specification (and any bills of quantities) are offered to one contractor and prices are negotiated directly with the quantity surveyor.
4. *Cost plus an agreed percentage* – an agreement to pay a contractor at rates which are recognized to be at cost and an agreed percentage of profit added.

   5. *Cost plus a fixed fee* – an agreement to pay a contractor at rates which are recognized to be at cost and a fixed fee added.

Making a choice is not as simple as it might seem. The operational intricacies and ramifications of choosing one possibility is where the quantity surveyor's advice is needed.

○     *Advises about the type of contract which the client and contractor may enter into.*

— Assists with choosing a standard form of contract from the range available.

— Advises about the type of contract which will best suit the type of project to be undertaken: whether it is for normal building work, package deal work, civil engineering work, use of industrialized systems, or providing for a series of similar projects.

○     *Compiles and supplies bills of quantities and particulars for combining with the architect's drawings and specification.*

— Collaborates throughout the detailed design stages, supplying cost advice to the architect and other members of the design team about all aspects of the building, its engineering, site and fittings.

— Predicts the value of tender to expect by pricing the bills of quantities before tenders are invited.

During the working drawing stage a quantity surveyor produces updated costed plans, obtains quotations for subcontracted work and nominated suppliers' items, makes preliminary enquiries about suitable contractors, prepares a preliminary list of firms from which to invite competitive tenders, and after receipt of tenders will check the prices received and report to the architect and the client.

○     *Deals with all financial matters during the construction phase and after the project is completed.*

— Measures and agrees cost of any variation to the building with the contractor.

— Prepares interim valuations of all completed work for the architect to use as a basis for certifying how much money the client is due to pay to the contractor.

— Prepares and issues quarterly financial statements to keep the client informed.

— Prepares a final account of the full project cost for agreement with the contractor which forms the basis of the architect's final certification of payment due to the contractor.

During and when the project is completed, the quantity surveyor is responsible for assessing correctly the value of the constructed work, in the form of either interim or final statements. Because a quantity surveyor's work is imperceptible in the finished building, his special contribution should never be lost sight of or undervalued.

### 5.5.3 The environmental engineer

○   *Advises about broad engineering matters affecting the site services, interior environment and engineering installations.*
— Becomes involved in those parts of the project for which he has the appropriate technical knowledge and experience.
— Conducts technical surveys, appraisals and feasibility studies into requirements of spaceheating, daylighting, artificial illumination or ventilation.

○   *Evaluates environmental conditions and advises about the various engineering alternatives available.*
— Recommends engineering solutions to interior environmental problems encountered within the building or concerning its services.

It pays to involve environmental engineers when briefing begins and when alternative sites or buildings are being examined. When they are present at meetings, they bring to attention the necessity of thinking about environmental possibilities and alternatives. Their presence also leads to a degree of realism at this stage of the project.

○   *Helps define his responsibilities to the client and architect.*
— Confirms with the architect which elements of the environmental design he will work on.
— States any limitations to his responsibility.
— Agrees to act as consultant to the architect, *or*
— Agrees to be responsible direct to the client whilst cooperating with the architect, and acting under his direction as team leader.

As the initial designs firm up and the engineering design services which are required become clearer, it is possible to define which installations the structural engineer should work on. This is the time to decide who does what, and draw up agreements with the client or architect.

○   *Probes and elucidates the environmental implications of elements of the brief and initial designs.*
— Receives and analyses the brief and architectural design drawings and provides an engineering response through the design phase.

○   *Interprets and applies engineering standards, regulations and codes of practice in direct support of his own work.*
— Applies up-to-date regulations and codes of practice to the project.

Engaging environmental engineers does more than insure against problems with the internal environment. With detailed knowledge of the characteristics of spaceheating, lighting and ventilation systems and the techniques of integrating them with the building design, they can help with the choice of workable methods and arrangements from the outset. This reduces overall design time. Also, because they are conversant with relevant legislation, delays which could arise from any non-compliance with building regulations are virtually eliminated.

o   *Supplies full engineering designs and particulars for combining with the architect's drawings.*

— Collaborates throughout the design stages, supplying designs and advice in drawn or descriptive form to the architect and all specialist contractors and manufacturers.

o   *Supplies detail designs for fabrication and installation of specialist items of equipment and fittings.*

— At the working drawing stage an environmental engineer produces detailed drawings, specification clauses and critical dimensions of elements of spaceheating, electrical or ventilation schemes which become integrated, first into the set of working drawings, and then into the building itself.

An environmental engineer is responsible for the advice he gives and the effective operation of his engineering designs and specifications, but cannot be held accountable if the architect has curtailed or modified his work.

Because the results of environmental engineering work is so keenly felt by the people using the finished building, this aspect of building design should never be overlooked when the brief is being compiled.

### 5.5.4 The planning supervisor

The responsibilities of the planning officer defined by the CDM Regulations apply whether the project architect accepts the additional appointment or whether another architect or professional is appointed. These are:

o   *Gives notice to the Health and Safety Executive.*

— The Health and Safety Executive considers that a project exists from the earliest design stage. It must receive formal notice as soon as the project commences.

o   *Checks that all appointed designers and other consultants have carefully considered all aspects of health and safety in their design work.*

— Discusses building design details and procedures with the design team, including safe access for subsequent repair and maintenance.

— Reviews possible hazards and forseeable risks in construction work so that the designers can combat them when designing.

— Encourages the use of risk assessment procedures, in order to identify and eliminate, or avoid, all risks.

○      *Ensures a Health and Safety Plan is prepared.*
—    Receives material from all involved in the design process as it takes place.
—    Checks and ensures the compilation is amplified to give warning of hazards peculiar to the project.
—    Ensures the principal contractor develops the plan by contributing health and safety matters affecting the construction phase.
—    Coordinates and edits all material received into a coherent, comprehensive document which meets the requirements of the CDM Regulations.
—    Advises the client that it is clear for construction work to begin when a satisfactory Health and Safety Plan is ready.

The purpose of the Health and Safety Plan is to highlight for the contractor all forseeable hazards which could arise during the construction phase. It is important that time is made available for this work to be done.

○      *Ensures a Health and Safety File is prepared and delivered to the client when the building is finished.*
—    Obtains details of the building and its installations and equipment from the architect, consultants, contractor, subcontractors, and all manufacturers and suppliers involved in the project.
—    Compiles a single file which focuses particularly on health and safety aspects of the materials used and also design implications for those who subsequently work on the building.

This Health and Safety File is intended to provide contractors engaged in the future to adapt, extend, refurbish or repair the building, with a single reliable point of reference to alert them about parts of the structure, or materials and finishes which could be hazardous to work on. Apart from records of construction methods and materials used, as-built drawings, and technical operating manuals for all equipment and specialist installations, the File would provide recommendations for routine maintenance and cleaning and details of fire protection measures and security installations.

# How to organize and manage briefing

**Be sure you can avoid the pitfalls and set-backs which could hinder the production of a brief and disrupt the project timetable!**

Key components of a method of working are set out in this section as a practical guide to help with:

o    Setting up the design team and agreeing how to communicate with each other.

o    Making arrangements to be sure the brief and sketch plans are produced correctly and efficiently.

o    Setting up a timetable.

o    The client's contribution: essential tasks which a client must be sure to carry out.

When ready to begin, all brief writers are faced with difficulties which could hinder the production of a brief. These are:

o    Not knowing how or where to start.

o    Losing a sense of what to do next.

o    Not knowing when to seek decisions or responses from colleagues or the consultants.

o    Not knowing how much time and resources to set aside to deal properly with the briefing activities.

Also there is a real concern about how to compose the brief and organize its production. Fortunately there is a *modus operandi* which experienced architects use, often quite instinctively. It is adapted to suit the project type and the experience of the client. The key

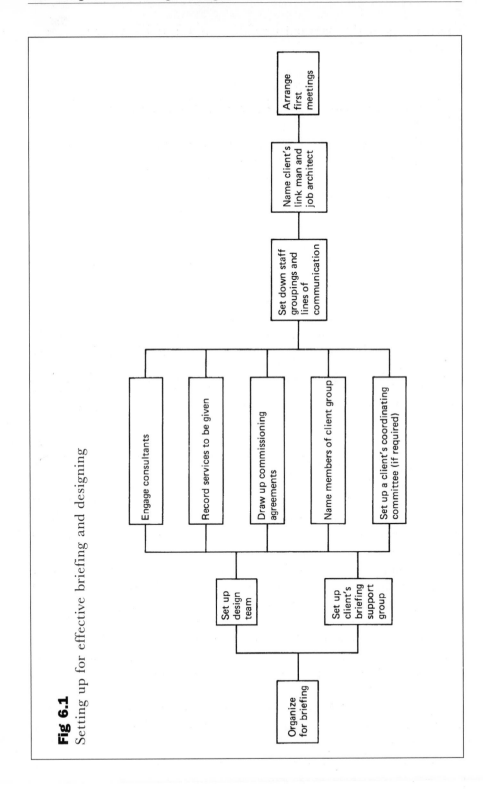

**Fig 6.1**
Setting up for effective briefing and designing

components of this method provide a useful and reassuring frame-work within which to work.

## 6.1    Setting up an effective organization for smooth working

It is first necessary for the client and design team to decide how they will relate to each other. They need to ask:
○      Are we properly set up as a design team?
○      How do we intend to communicate?
○      How will we keep track of the information which is to pass between us?
○      How will we control what is going on?
○      Do we understand each other's organization and proposed methods well enough?
○      What will our operational framework be?
○      How will we coordinate our efforts?
To manage the briefing process effectively, both the client and the architect need to know what has to be done about all these things and what is possible. Also they both need to take firm control of the management of their own team and their activities. An outline of necessary steps is set out in Section 6.3.

## 6.2    Setting up a timetable of operations

At an early stage it is well worthwhile drawing up a time schedule to establish all the stages which need to be worked through and the probable time involved. A simple bar chart can be used to present the timetable, similar to the illustration given in Fig 6.2.

Be as realistic as possible when preparing a timetable of opera-tions. It can then be used to plan the availability of resources such as designer's time, and staff time to appraise and approve designs and costs. It will also help determine key dates, such as when to submit planning and building regulation applications to be sure they coincide with local council meetings, or ensure legal possession of the site is obtained in good time for the contractor to start site works.

The timetable will inevitably need updating periodically. However, any adjustments needed will show how other related activi-ties will be affected and will allow a complete review of the whole project timetable to be made as well as its parts.

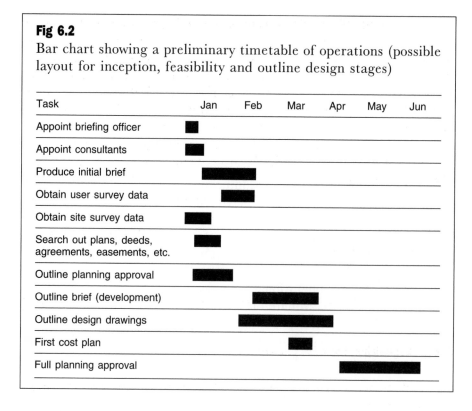

**Fig 6.2**

Bar chart showing a preliminary timetable of operations (possible layout for inception, feasibility and outline design stages)

| Task | Jan | Feb | Mar | Apr | May | Jun |
|---|---|---|---|---|---|---|
| Appoint briefing officer | ▮ | | | | | |
| Appoint consultants | ▮ | | | | | |
| Produce initial brief | ▬▬ | | | | | |
| Obtain user survey data | ▬ | | | | | |
| Obtain site survey data | ▮ | | | | | |
| Search out plans, deeds, agreements, easements, etc. | ▮ | | | | | |
| Outline planning approval | ▬ | | | | | |
| Outline brief (development) | | ▬▬ | | | | |
| Outline design drawings | | ▬▬▬ | | | | |
| First cost plan | | | ▮ | | | |
| Full planning approval | | | | | ▬▬ | |

## 6.3    A checklist for use by the client when getting organized for briefing

### 6.3.1    Setting up the design team

o    Ensure that all necessary professional persons or firms have been selected to give a complete service suited to the project in hand, e.g. architect, engineers, project manager, quantity surveyor, interior designer, landscape architect.

o    Check their experience, competence and the likelihood of their proving compatible and being fully committed to your project.

o    Check that appointments are clearly made and agreements promptly drawn up. (Obtain forms of agreement and guidance notes from the relevant professional institutions.)

o    Be quite sure that the responsibilities of each consultant are fully agreed and documented.

o    Check that the architect has been given express authority to act as the team leader (or the project manager, if one is engaged).

o    Involve your architect, or project manager, in all actions you take from now on.

Do not be tempted to defer the selection and appointment of a consultant until a later stage. 'I want to be quite sure there is substantial work to do which warrants engaging a specialist consultant,' the client may say. If there is a doubt, undertake a preliminary agreement for limited services only and extend it later. Forming the full design team at the beginning ensures that all legal, physical and economic aspects of the project can be developed in step with one another from the beginning.

Exploring the standard commissioning agreement forms supplied by the professional institutions will help to define responsibilities. Optional services will be found which may, or may not, be required. For example, a structural engineer may be commissioned to produce structural designs and detailed working drawings, but not to supervise the work on site. This is also the time to settle the question of expenses and other ongoing costs, such as:

o   Costs of extra copies of drawings.

o   Travel and subsistence costs.

o   Any hourly rates to be agreed, particularly those of principals and partners.

### 6.3.2   Organizing the client group

o   Identify and name members of the client group. Indicate their responsibilities.

o   If overall responsibility cannot be concentrated in one person, appoint a committee for collective decision making.

o   Allocate administrative and advisory support to the team.

o   Produce a simple diagram to explain the internal relationships of the client group for the information of everyone in the client's organization and the design team.

o   Allocate and name a single person as spokesman or link man with the design team – a briefing or liaison officer.

o   If a large organization with specialists on the staff, set down clear directives about their role. They should do no more than help with the preparation of the brief and assess the design team's proposals – even if architects, engineers or quantity surveyors. They should not blur the design team's responsibilities.

o   Hold an in-house meeting to inform everyone involved about their responsibilities and extent of their contribution to the briefing activities. At this meeting define how and who to communicate with.

A client cannot do his part of the briefing job well unless he has organized himself and his staff to do so.

A governing factor affecting the form of the client team is the size and complexity of the project. If small, one or two managers or directors would prove adequate. They would need an administrator and would need to be able to call on legal or technical advisers. If a large or complicated project, the client team should include representatives of all departments or groups responsible for managing, financing and using the building, as well as advisers for legal, technical or professional matters.

Coordinating committees become vital when the client organization is particularly large and made up of separate, widely dispersed departments or units. If the people forming the client's briefing team do not work in the same office block, near enough to make daily contact a natural thing, then frequent working meetings should be planned to ensure that they communicate regularly. Some of their meetings would need to be planned for the purpose of coordinating all contributions – policy, opinions, data and decisions affecting the project – and involving outside organizations, such as financiers, government departments or associated companies with an interest.

### 6.3.3 Developing an understanding with the design team about staff groupings and systems of working

o    Whilst completing arrangements to commission the architect, or setting up surveys or feasibility studies:
—    Arrange special visits to the design team's offices to see their methods at first hand.
—    Invite design team members to visit your offices for the same purpose.
o    Ask for names and responsibilities of each member of the architect's staff who is to work with you.
o    Establish clearly who is the partner or architect in charge of the project.
o    Ask who is to be the link on behalf of the design team (it won't necessarily be the same person).
o    Ask to be shown examples of documents and drawings you are not conversant with. Find out the differences between sketch plans and scheme design drawings.
o    Be sure you know how the architect conducts the cost planning of the project.
Try to get beyond any 'front' which may be presented to you by the firm, partnership or organization you are to work with. Individuals and their particular roles and responsibilities should eventually become well known to you and your staff. If you are to work closely together, a formal 'front' should not exist.

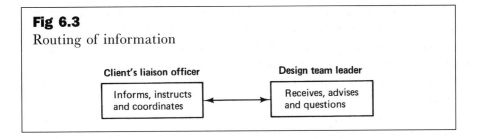

**Fig 6.3**
Routing of information

### 6.3.4  Setting up lines of communication

o     Arrange for transfer of data, and requests for information and all decisions to be routed directly between the nominated representatives of the client and the architect (Fig 6.3).

o     Clarify the composition of both the client team and design team, and note down lines of communication. Prepare a simple diagram for agreement (see Fig 6.4).

o     Ensure that staff groupings are not too elaborate.

o     Include a representative of the ultimate building user in some way.

If the client organization has any association or controlling body which can influence its policies, particularly financial policies, this should be disclosed to the design team and be indicated on the client network diagram. It is not a private matter for the client if an outside organization has the power to ask for the project to be halted, delayed or adjusted. For example, if the client is a local authority it may be necessary for reference to be made periodically to a government central or regional office for sanctions to progress through prescribed stages of the briefing and design work. If the architect knows about this organization and the powers and areas of influence it has, he can suggest times when informal contact might usefully be made to clarify particular points which might ultimately prove contentious and disrupt the project timetable.

### 6.3.5  Setting up a means of collecting and recording data affecting the building and its site

o     *Establish a documentation system appropriate to the project size.* This is to aid the assembly of a brief and managing the process of briefing. There are a number of work books, schedules and proformas which should be obtained and brought into use immediately. Details of these and appropriate documentation methods are given in Chapter 7.

o    *Set up a computer-based method of assembling and organizing the information which will make up the brief.* A practical method of writing, recording and updating the brief is to use a personal computer or word processor linked to a printer. Most organizations are equipped and have staff expert enough to operate such a system. This method is available to any individual commissioning building work who is personally experienced in word processing.

o    *Organize joint client/architect visits to recently completed buildings of similar type.* This can be time well spent. When the client group and design organization look closely together at features of existing buildings, new and old, their reactions trigger off a number of very useful events.

—    The experience stimulates and strengthens the ability of the client group to imagine the effect of room relationships and the use of space in their own project: for example, the client may know at a glance that the shape and height of an assembly hall is quite wrong for his purposes, and would also be able to explain why.

—    A tour of a building can precipitate discussion about aspects of the brief which might otherwise never have been raised or written into the brief: for example, a client team requiring a library building, when first walking into the entrance areas of a recently occupied library, immediately noticed smells of cooking from a small cafeteria situated nearby – something they quite clearly did not want!

—    It is a very useful way for the client and designer groups to get to know each other, their aspirations and general attitudes to the design opportunities before them – a first step in building up a good working relationship.

—    It provides opportunities to see people in their living, recreation or workspaces using their equipment and fittings, and to observe the conditions which surround them – there is no substitute for first-hand observation of this kind.

—    It helps develop a common appreciation of standards.

### 6.3.6   Providing for effective overall management of the project

o    Identify who is to be responsible for overall project management and for managing the production of the brief and sketch plans.

o    Decide whether this is best done by the architect or consultant who is leading the project design team.

o    Otherwise appoint a project manager to act as a separate consultancy responsible directly to the client organization.

### 6.3.7  Checking on any previous actions about the site, building and policy decisions

o      Collect together an historical record of any decisions already made concerning the project.

o      Search for any notices received in the past or any agreements which may have been entered into prior to the commencement of the project which could affect use of the site or existing buildings – easements, tenancies, dangerous structure notices or leases.

### 6.3.8  Utilizing formal and informal working methods

o      Ensure that members of the client group are alerted about the uses and appropriateness of formal and informal methods of communication with the designers.

o      Because this subject is so important, time should be taken to inform all people involved in the briefing work when to act formally or informally, and highlight the consequences of using the wrong method. Informal and relaxed relationships tend to develop naturally when the interdependent nature of the briefing work becomes clear to the people involved. Uncertainties fade away and ideas are offered and discussed more freely in an informal atmosphere. Because informality can enhance and magnify the client's representatives' contribution to discussions about the brief and preliminary designs, it is of high value.

However informal and relaxed a relationship the client group might establish when they work closely with the design team members, they should clearly understand the different characteristics of formal and informal methods of working.

#### *Informality*

o      Individuals freely talk to each other without passing information through the recognized link route (client's briefing officer to the design team leader).

o      This is a very good method of creating a working environment which allows quick responses and the offering up of ideas, facts or knowledge which might not otherwise be passed to the design team.

o      It can produce vague or inaccurate data which should be carefully verified later.

o      It is most useful when trying to open up a range of possibilities in the early design stage.

o      Decisions usually take place 'off the record' and so can prove difficult to record. They may never appear in the brief.

o      Informality should not be the norm.

*Formality*

o     This involves using the normal method of routing information through to the design team leader. Individuals pass data and ideas to the designers through the briefing officer.

o     If an individual knows an informal communication of some consequence has occurred, details of the information or decision made should be notified to the briefing officer for inclusion in a formal document of instruction to the architect or consultant.

Take care always to confirm the information given and the decisions arrived at when individuals from the client group and design team work informally together – either in meetings or over the telephone. The client's formal instruction route to the design team leader should never be side-stepped or forgotten.

### 6.3.9   Preparing a project timetable

o     Prepare a comprehensive timetable of operations with the architect or project manager.

o     Use the periods which the architect considers necessary to adequately deal with each stage of the project:
  —   Briefing and initial design.
  —   Sketch designs.
  —   Preparation of working drawings and contract particulars.
  —   Construction period on site.

o     Determine whether the desired completion date for the project is feasible.

o     Adjust the timetable in conjunction with the architect.

o     Ensure that sufficient time is provided for the briefing operation and for thoroughly comprehending and understanding the demands to be made on the building.

Time is important. Timetabling should be seen as a means of organizing and managing the time available. Used correctly, it can help to coordinate effort and create a climate of enthusiasm by setting realistic work targets.

It is natural for the client to want to have the construction work begun at the earliest possible moment. A construction start date is usually the time which is uppermost in the client's mind. However, should a site start be made prematurely, that is without the working drawings being properly completed, ensuing problems, such as delays, additional costs and unsatisfactory work, are inevitable.

Time spent settling the brief and agreeing a timetable is necessary if the client is to obtain best value for money, and the architect achieve a well worked-out, trouble-free building of lasting value.

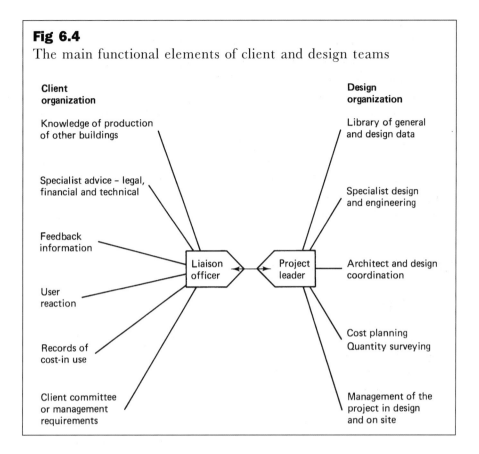

**Fig 6.4**

The main functional elements of client and design teams

## 6.4    The main functional elements of client and design teams

The client's liaison officer and the designer's project leader must be skilful enough to perform all the functions in Fig 6.4, or must be able to call on others to do them and coordinate the contributions. Both organizations will:

o    Embrace some of the knowledge and skills shown here.

o    Hold records about some of them.

o    Either employ staff or engage outside firms or consultants to perform each function; *OR*

o    Include all functions within one or two persons representing a small client or professional practice.

Check that you are able to draw on all the knowledge and skills indicated above. If you have not got the knowledge and data yourself, or employ partly qualified or inexperienced staff, and do not retain advisers and consultants to help you, take steps to fill in the gaps.

## 6.5    Overriding activities for the client

The client or the people making up the client's briefing group have a number of fundamental activities which are theirs alone. These activities must be done if briefing is to happen. They cannot be done by an architect or project manager. Some of them may be delegated.

o    *Directing the project.*
   — Have an overview.
   — Initiate action and maintain momentum.
o    *Thinking out need.*
   — Think out what is needed.
   — Test, decide and evaluate.
   — Think ahead.
o    *Selection of ideas and data.*
   — Select between options.
   — Discover alternative routes, possibilities and opportunities.
o    *Finding out.*
   — Find out realistically what can be afforded, in what position, for which user.
   — Find out the legal position and any grants available.
   — Research site, finances available and any constraints.
o    *Expressing and implementing.*
   — Set down requirements, limits, demands, opportunities, for instructing the architect.
o    *Transmitting and receiving.*
   — Pass instructions, information and decisions to the architect and design team.
   — Listen to questions and requests for information.
   — Be prepared to respond and become organized to do so.
o    *Recording.*
   — Keep own notes and vital data.
   — Compile and record the brief.
   — Update as necessary.

## 6.6    Management of the project

Overall management of a project is usually undertaken by the archi-
te~t. It is more than a matter of overseeing everything needed to
   ‘nister the contract and progress and complete the building.
   ıgh regarded in the past as a natural part of the architect's
      \ to a client, the task has grown considerably and is now seen
       ‘screte service attracting a separate fee and requiring specific

professional indemnity cover, especially when highly complex projects are involved.

Large, costly buildings, or those constructed of very high quality materials are not necessarily complex in management terms and not all of them would present an unusually difficult management problem. More than usual management skills are needed to organize and run projects when tight time constraints are imposed, or where an unusual number of consultants or user groups are taking part, or when a multiplicity of industrial processes are involved in the construction of a building. Under these circumstances the client might consider it worthwhile to appoint a project manager. For example, when the project is part of a large-scale comprehensive site development scheme which embraces a number of different building or engineering projects for more than one client organization, then an independent project manager is undoubtably needed. A site development supremo makes sense in this case.

### 6.6.1   Deciding who can adopt the role of project manager

The decision to appoint an *independent* consultant as project manager should not be made without considering all possibilities. For the majority of projects, appointing a separate specialist consultant may not be necessary at all.

Options are:

o      The client, or a member of the client organization, undertakes the role.

o      The architect is engaged and undertakes the role as a separate appointment.

o      An independent project manager is appointed.

Whoever takes on the role, whether an individual or a firm, should be highly experienced in the working methods and problems of the professional and contracting specialisms which predominate in the construction industry. Also, he should be keenly aware of the manner in which design work is carried out and the way in which a workable built form is evolved. Knowledge of essential planning procedures and, of course, skill and experience in managing construction projects is vital.

When deciding who is to manage the project, including the briefing and design stages, the purpose and objectives of the management work should dictate. These are, of course, to ultimately produce a building which is satisfactory in every way – perfectly meeting all the client's requirements, within the expected time and cost, and also the demands of the users and any visiting public.

To meet these objectives, everyone's efforts in producing a brief must run smoothly, without hold-ups or going over the same ground twice; all the preparatory research, decision making and design work should be completed within the time-span allotted and nothing overlooked or omitted.

As overseeing these operations might appear to be basically non-technical, the overall management task could be considered to fall naturally within the capacity of highly trained and experienced managers of almost any background. But ideally a project manager should be experienced in the art of designing and organizing the production of the information needed for the construction of buildings and be equipped with enough experience to know instinctively how to overcome obstacles raised against the project from sources outside the client and design teams. It is important that the project manager possesses the skill to anticipate problems which may arise, and how best to counter them.

### 6.6.2  Strategies for project management

Setting up and directing the project is very much the client's concern, as is the ultimate responsibility for all major decisions taken. In view of this, the client might consider undertaking the whole of the project management task. Can this be done? And what alternatives are there?

o      *Can the client, or a member of a client organization, take on the role of project manager?*
If the person involved is basically a strategist and enabler and has the experience outlined in Section 6.6.1 and can be released from all other commitments within the client organization, then it is possible. But the salary costs and other supporting operational costs to the organization need to be compared to the cost of engaging the architect or a separate outside consultant.

o      *Should the architect engaged on the project act as project manager?*
Normally architects are best placed to act as project manager. Their training and experience brings to each project an insight and aware-ness into how the client can clarify his aspirations and organize the means of defining realizable requirements in a brief. Also, with devel-oped skills in motivating and cooperating with engineers and other designers to produce coherent project designs, they are well qualified to take on the role of project manager.

If clients have any doubts about their architect's abilities and competence as a project manager, they may soon be able to make assessments. The architectural profession is taking steps to register practices and individual architects who have undertaken and passed prescribed training and refresher courses. Also, an industry-wide accreditation system is being devised in the UK by a number of professional bodies including the Royal Institute of British Architects.

○       *Is it best to appoint a completely independent consultant specializing in project management?*

Take this step only if there are strong reasons not to adopt either of the previous options. It is generally thought not to be in the best interests of the client to load another tier of management onto the design team. The appointment can introduce a potential barrier to the free relationship of the client with his consultants.

The appointment should only be made when the project is complicated enough to make sense of the idea of relieving the architect and other design team members from complex organizational demands which could detract from their design functions. It becomes best practice when a project is seen to have a number of special constraints, such as a taxing set of legislative procedures to meet, an exacting critical timescale, or demands from a multiplicity of client and user organizations who wish to make an input to the realization of the project.

# The process of briefing

o      The sequence of activities and things which have to be thought about.

o      The parts of the brief.

o      An outline of initiatives which the various people involved can take on.

o      Reading and interpreting architects' drawings.

o      Decisions which the client is expected to make during the early design stage.

*client + Archited of brief what need*

## 7.1     The parts of the brief – basic requirements for a building

The list below sets out the basic requirements of almost any building project. It is given here so that a brief writer can use it as a prompt to suggest the items which he might wish to give instructions about. One of the uses an architect might have for it will be to check that nothing vital is omitted from the client's brief.

Another use for this table is to help draw up agendas or lists for discussions between the client and the design team.

| *List of basic requirements* | *CI/SfB Table 4 reference* |
| --- | --- |
| *Policy* – basic purpose and function of the project; organizational structure; management needs; communication systems required to service the proposed activities and organization, telecommunications. | (A) |

## Fig 7.1

Method of producing a brief using the basic requirements list

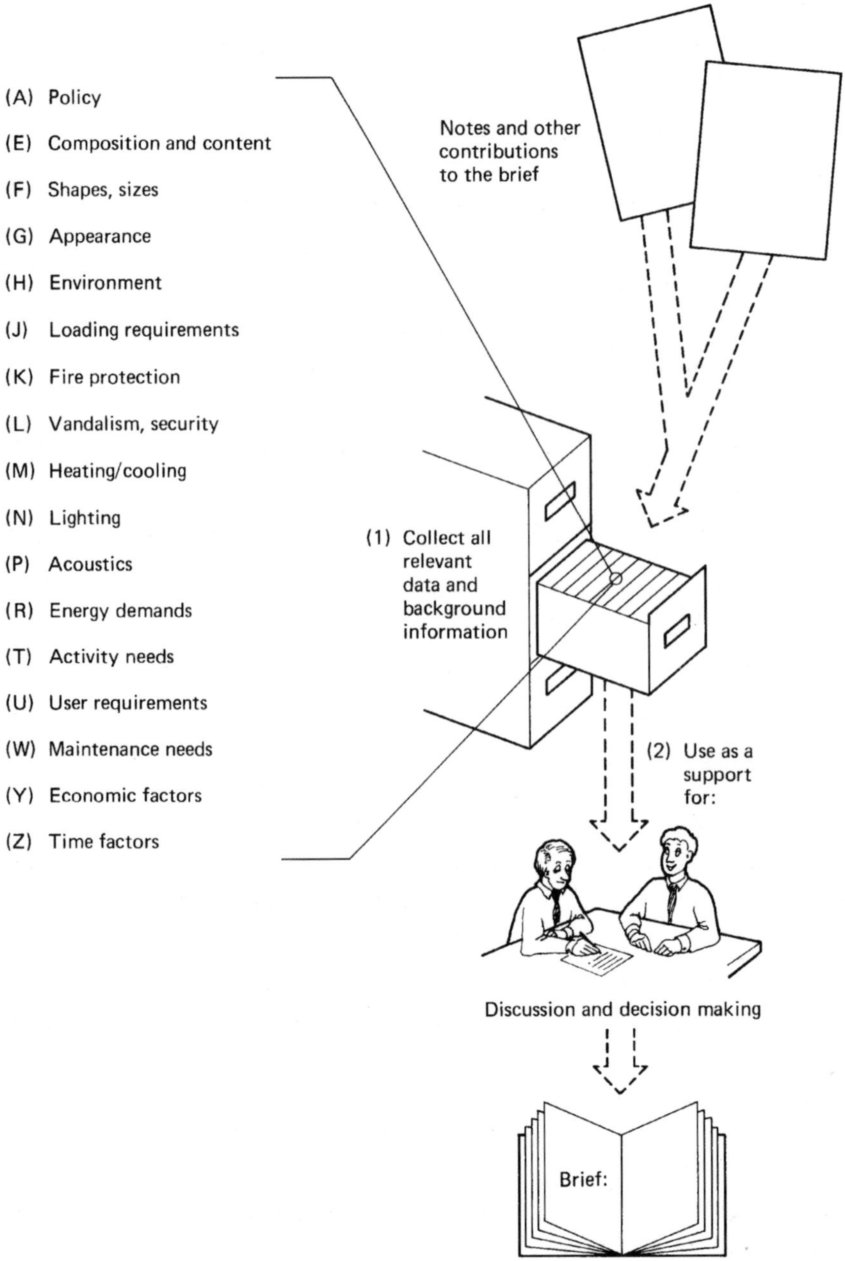

(A)  Policy

(E)  Composition and content

(F)  Shapes, sizes

(G)  Appearance

(H)  Environment

(J)  Loading requirements

(K)  Fire protection

(L)  Vandalism, security

(M)  Heating/cooling

(N)  Lighting

(P)  Acoustics

(R)  Energy demands

(T)  Activity needs

(U)  User requirements

(W)  Maintenance needs

(Y)  Economic factors

(Z)  Time factors

Notes and other contributions to the brief

(1) Collect all relevant data and background information

(2) Use as a support for:

Discussion and decision making

Brief:

*Composition and content* – description of constituent parts; elements and functions; departments; suites; relationships; specific groupings. (E)

*Shapes and sizes* – accommodation schedule and sizes, critical dimensions, areas. (F)

*Appearance* – factors relating to preferred form, scale, texture, colour, proportion and style (if any). (G)

*Environment* – factors relating to surroundings; occupancy needs; amenities; type and quality of internal and external environment; internal and external landscaping. (H)

*Loading requirements* – superimposed loads, wind loads; acceptable limits of structural deformation. (J)

*Fire protection* – legislative requirements; means of escape; fire-fighting installations and equipment; spread of flame prevention. (K)

*Contamination protection* – ventilation; humidity; proofing against contamination and damages; security installations. (L)

*Heating/cooling* – thermal factors, temperature requirements. (M)

*Lighting* – natural and artificial lighting requirements; emergency lighting; display lighting. (N)

*Acoustics* – factors affecting sound attenuation; sound insulation. (P)

*Energy demands* – services required; standby systems; solar energy requirements. (R)

*Activity needs* – specific activities to be accommodated; circulation factors governing layouts and levels; pedestrian and vehicular traffic and access; working methods; equipment; lifts, hoists, staircases, ramps; type of plant employed and method of operation. (T)

*User requirements* – sociological factors and user description (as groups or individuals); staff categories and management structure; degree of flexibility required. (U)

*Maintenance needs* – maintenance programme demands; quality of structure, materials and installations, vacuum points, cradles. (W)

*Economic factors* – client's financial resources; limits of capital costs and costs-in-use. (Y)

*Time factors* – time limits; design and construction programme. (Z)

The headings and definitions which make up the table have been taken from the *Architect's Job Book*, 1977 Revision, published by the Royal Institute of British Architects. (See 'List of basic requirements of a total project' on page B3.2.)

CI/SfB References are those given in the *CI/SfB Construction Indexing Manual* published by RIBA Services Limited, a subsidiary company of the Royal Institute of British Architects. These codes are particularly useful for filing and retrieval purposes, especially when data is to be stored by a computer system.

## 7.2  General sequence of activities

Successfully implementing the briefing and design of a building project depends largely upon being able to put in hand a general sequence of initiatives. They continuously affect both the client and architect and are interdependent in nature.

The chart on p. 117 illustrates these initiatives in simple outline form. They form a thread which runs through each of the work stages from inception to completion of scheme design. In practice, the activities being initiated can cycle back through earlier work stages and are used many times over.

If these initiatives are not kept up, lapses can occur in the interaction of the client and design teams, eventually resulting in a loss of momentum and possibly the missing of an important deadline in the project timetable. Days lost in the briefing and initial design stage will impact on the date when the building can be occupied, and, therefore, involve some financial loss to the client.

## 7.3  The process of briefing – what actually happens

Often clients ask, 'What actually happens when a brief is compiled?' and 'What exactly am I expected to do?'

Successful briefing depends entirely upon how well the client and architect both fulfil their parts in the process; how informed they are and how skilful they are.

The part each plays is set out below. It is divided into four sections representing the four stages of work which briefing and design goes through on normal building projects. These stages of work are those set out in the *Plan of Work for Design Team Operations* published by the Royal Institute of British Architects (see Chapter 3):

## Sequence of initiatives

**1.** Client's initiative      conceiving      aims

| | | |
|---|---|---|
| | collecting | objectives |
| | recording | image |
| | collating | philosophy |
| | coordinating | values |
| | weighing | attitudes |
| | balancing | user needs |
| | consulting | standards |
| | deciding | facts |
| | *and:* | |

*Communicating the result to the design team*
    (usually briefing material)

**2.** Architect's initiative      receiving

                                           assimilating
                                           comprehending
                                           understanding
                                           testing
                                           interpreting
                                           *and:*

*Presenting the result to the client group*
    (usually diagrammatic illustrations, sketches or reports of
    possibilities)

**3.** Client's initiative      appraising

                                             checking
                                             amending
                                             consulting
                                             deciding
                                             *and:*

*Communicating the result to the design team*
    (usually responses and more information for the brief)

**4.** Architect's initiative      developing

                                             recasting
                                             *and:*

*Presenting the result to the client group*
    (usually sketches or design drawings)

**5.** Client's initiative      appraising

                                             accepting
                                             approving
                                             *and:*

*Issuing instructions for the project to proceed to working drawing stage*

A. *Inception* – when a general idea of what is needed is identified.

B. *Feasibility* – when testing and reviewing of the first ideas takes place.

C. *Outline proposals* – when design sketches begin to clarify and the brief develops.

D. *Scheme design* – when interaction and reaction further develop the brief and a firm design solution emerges.

### 7.3.1   The briefing process (stage A): inception

#### Objective
o      To produce a general statement defining what is needed in the building project, including:
— Aims and requirements.
— The activities to be accommodated.
— Any organizational grouping required.
— Numbers of people involved.
— First notions of dimensions, areas and spaces.
o      To inform the architect sufficiently for realistic feasibility studies to commence.

#### Client's first activities
**1.** Write down or sketch out your first ideas about what is needed. Put down the ideas as they come. Leave the organization of the material until a later stage.
o      You may only produce a list of notes with a diagram or two, but these will serve as prompts for the first working meeting with the architect.
o      Anything you think of as vitally important should be included at this time.
o      If you have a completed building in mind and intend to use it as a model for your own building, take care. Your notes will tend to say, '. . . as the High Street Offices but . . .' and will really be a list of differences and modifications to that building. This can indicate to an architect how you are thinking, but it is not the best way to begin briefing.
o      In the case of factory units and extensions, include details of items to be housed, any special equipment or plant and how it is to be operated.
o      Attach copies of any records you may have concerning the site (or existing building): estate agent's details, existing plans and agreements or previously obtained approvals.
**2.** Concentrate first on setting down the things which you feel will shape the overall form of the building; deal with your aims and with

the people and activities which will occupy it. Afterwards add more detailed data about room layouts, fittings and the environmental services which are preferred – all those factors which will shape the interior, but have less impact on the overall building form.

o      What the client is required to deal with first are fundamental matters of strategic importance. Describe details about occupancy rather than how it is accommodated. (A checklist of possible items is given on p. 155.)

o      Items such as types of partitioning, artificial lighting requirements, furniture and machine layouts are secondary at this time.

o      Highlight aims and occupancy requirements which have the highest priority – anything which would render the building useless if not fulfilled. Also state any items included in the brief which are optional or uncertain.

**3.** If you have a brief for another similar building to work from it is still better practice to prepare an independent statement of your own; but also supply a copy of the brief you are working from to the architect for his information.

o      It is incorrect to assume that amending a brief for another building will produce a building which entirely satisfies the client and building users. It is also very limiting. It suggests that everything the architect needs to know is already described and that there is very little else to think about. What he really needs to know at this stage are the client's aims and priorities.

o      Some large client organizations will possess a reference brief for buildings which they commission frequently. This would be available and be passed to the architect, but in addition to and not instead of a specific project brief.

o      Clients with previous experience, large commercial and industrial organizations, government and local government departments also provide design notes and procedural guidance at this stage.

**4.** Transfer your preliminary description and all the available information and plans to the architect.

o      Ideally, this should be done at a meeting when any key points or questions can be clarified immediately.

o      After this meeting send further thoughts, ideas or questions to the architect as soon as they come to mind.

o      Always respond to his queries promptly.

**5.** Put in hand a survey of the site (or existing building and its surrounds) if you have not already done so.

o      Usually the architect or consultant leading the project will carry out a measured survey of the site, its boundaries and features including levels and all services.

### Architect's first activities

**1.** Collect and record all the information received and rearrange it for the purpose of examining the feasibility of the project.

o     Usually the information received is diverse and tentative, and could range from sparse notes of vital strategic points to quantities of highly detailed descriptions of particular known needs.

**2.** Look through the information and extract facts which are most relevant to the early stages of briefing and design.

o     Most architects prefer to have only those facts before them which are most appropriate to the particular stage being worked on. If material for a brief is weighty and complete in all details, it can inculcate a rigid approach which tends to restrict a flexible, open attitude when thinking about the design problems. It might even stifle imagination and originality. Hence the necessity to isolate and extract the most pertinent facts.

**3.** Discover and note down items not mentioned by the client. Glean from the site data and visits to the site, critical points which will influence the overall form of the project.

o     One method would be to refer to published records of similar building types; or to recollect something from previous professional experience and practice.

o     Initial design studies, the site analysis and initial feasibility exercises, will also reveal whether there are deficiencies in the briefing material received.

**4.** Draw out from the client further information and data to augment what has already been supplied. Assist him to identify all his requirements and those of the building users. Hold special meetings for this purpose.

o     Techniques which can help both the architect and the client with this task are for the architect to:

— Make suggestions about research or surveys which could be undertaken to determine user requirements.

— Highlight the main deciding factors which are influencing the arrangement or form of the building.

— Check whether there are uncertainties or difficulties which the client is experiencing in formulating the brief.

— Produce sketches and diagrams to illustrate options or possibilities which exist and which need the client's consideration.

### General comments

Before producing drawings of any kind an architect expects to absorb a great deal of background about:

o     The client and his organization.

o      The project need.
o      The site and its environment.
o      Similar completed buildings.

When responding to many probing questions and the inevitable suggestions which will be put forward, the client might feel that the project is not taking shape quickly enough. It is design sketches he will be eager to see. However, patient response and comment on ideas presented diagrammatically, or during meetings or visits to buildings, is really the most valuable contribution he can make at this stage.

Moving into the next stage of work, the feasibility stage, can happen very easily. It could go unnoticed. If a feasibility exercise is to be carried out, check that everyone concerned has done everything possible to finish this first stage of work – and be sure you agree with it.

### 7.3.2  The briefing process (stage B): testing the feasibility of the project and site

*Objective*

o      To produce design options and appraisals to ascertain whether the project as envisaged is feasible.
o      To prove the suitability and adequacy of the site and its features.
o      To study the practical implications of the demands being made on the likely form of the building and prove whether there are likely to be any constructional difficulties or severe technical problems to overcome.
o      To establish whether the client's idea of the project cost is achievable.
o      To help the client determine the form in which the project can proceed.
o      To check whether a clear way forward exists for the project.
o      To enable the client to continue confidently with developing the brief further.

*Client's activities*

**1.** Initiate and sanction feasibility studies to test important aspects of the project. Usual studies which are most likely to be needed are:
o      Investigating the site and available services – 'thumbnail' and diagrammatic sketches can be quickly produced to show how the building might be arranged and what influence the site constraints have on the building design.
o      Conducting investigations of subsoil conditions – this may involve engaging a structural engineer to examine the subsoils with auger or bore holes and recommend possible foundation types, structural solutions and engineering design criteria. If a choice of site has

not been made, this is the time to investigate their differences and the differing opportunities they offer.

o    Conducting financial appraisals for the sake of clarifying what the brief should include. Examples are:

— To indicate the comparative costs of alternative solutions to site engineering problems.

— To put a value on various preliminary design options when arranging the building on its site.

— To prove whether the finance earmarked for the project is enough.

o    Setting up user surveys – essential for important public buildings but useful for any project where the requirements of the people who are to use the building cannot be anticipated.

o    Checking the project timetable is feasible:

— Examining approvals already obtained and sought for the project, and for raising of loans and capital, to see if more should be done about securing them.

— Checking that submission dates and committee cycles for seeking town planning and other local authority approvals fit comfortably into the project timetable to reduce risk of delays.

**2.** Ask the architect to illustrate the effects of making changes to the outline brief to help you assess the relative importance of parts of the accommodation or some of your aims.

o    Here you need to be sure that the diagrams and other illustrations shown to you are understandable. If not, ask for further elaboration and explanation.

**3.** Respond quickly to requests from the architect for comments and appraisals of the feasibility exercises, and the initial design ideas being put forward.

o    In spite of their best intentions, clients, whether experienced or not, often find this a very difficult demand to meet. If you find you don't know how to respond, hold a working meeting with the architect. There will then be no lapse in the momentum of the design work.

o    Be sure you have the ability to respond quickly. It should be a priority activity.

o    Large client organizations should check that someone is given the authority to call on any member of the organization and its management for information and advice.

**4.** Do not allow feasibility studies to go on longer than needed to convince you that the brief is developing on the right lines. They can be costly in time and money, as feasibility studies attract an additional fee for the consultants involved. However, it is wise at this stage to investigate thoroughly every aspect of the project. Leaving this work undone can mean having to change the brief and possibly the designs at a later stage. It could even involve altering the building itself whilst under construction – the most expensive way there is to introduce changes.

o    Usually the architect will identify additional studies which are desirable, but it is for the client to agree that they are necessary.

o    Check whether additional fees will be involved to avoid misunderstandings arising later.

**5.** Receive a report from the architect on his findings, along with recommendations about how to proceed with the project.

o    The report could be verbal in the case of a very small, simple project, but more likely it will be a formal document setting out the architect's understanding of the site, any major obstacles or problems, and his ideas about how the main requirements of the brief may be developed into a viable building project.

o    If the client has not found out before, this is the time when he will discover whether the architect has understood all he has expressed. It is certainly the time to check that he has.

### Architect's activities

**1.** Studies the client's primary objectives and analyses the information which makes up the initial brief.

o    In so doing, the architect gradually assimilates the client's intentions. He will not feel able to produce realistic designs until he has absorbed the main requirements for the building.

**2.** Looks for any omissions or incompatible elements and seeks the client's assistance to clarify or resolve them.

o    This is a normal service of an architect. He will be more than eager to seek out what lies behind the information he has been given. He may use questionnaires, but he will invariably meet the client to talk more fully about what the brief entails.

o    He will also organize visits to completed buildings together with the client group to stimulate discussion and thought about what is needed.

**3.** Explores alternative approaches to finding a design solution.

o    Preliminary design sketches will be attempted to test out his ideas.

o    Options will be offered for appraisal and decision by the client.

**4.** Deepens his study of the client's requirements and recommends the feasibility studies required.

o    It may be necessary to demonstrate the value of undertaking special feasibility studies. They would normally be produced to assist a choice, or to indicate the potential of a site or a building.

o    Sometimes, a planning authority will require a preliminary design study to be done to illustrate the ultimate form of an extensive, comprehensive development scheme which includes a number of closely grouped buildings or engineering works, in addition to the client's building.

**5.** Reports his findings to the client.

o    Ideally this will be a written report. It is worth the architect taking the trouble to set down all the factors which influence the project as he sees it to ensure that the client has plenty of opportunity to study them.

### General comments

What happens during this stage of work is a widening of the view of everyone involved in the project. Both client and design group will:

o    Look outwards at all possible outside influences.

o    Search for the real needs of the client and users.

o    Discover the deciding factors affecting the overall arrangement and form of the proposed building.

In the process they should find they have grown together to function as a partnership.

Whilst this work goes on, the brief continues to grow. Many additions are made and ideas previously expressed become reshaped, altered and adjusted – a natural result of the active interrelationship of the client and design teams. The outcome will be either:

o    Being able to prove the viability of the project and the work done up to now on the brief; or

o    Discovering that the project needs radical adjustment, such as looking for another site, and restarting the appraisal and feasibility work.

### 7.3.3    The briefing process (stage C): whilst the outline sketch designs are produced

### Objective

o    To change the emphasis and content of the brief, using the results of the feasibility studies.

o    To firm up the main requirements of the brief and fill it out with more details concerning environmental and other internal require-ments and all external constraints.

o    To continually appraise the emerging designs to ensure they coincide with the brief.

o    To support the continuing design activities until a practical and acceptable outline plan emerges.

o    To arrive at a single general approach to the layout, design and method of constructing the project.

o    To consolidate the brief.

*Client's activities*

**1.** Consider the results of the feasibility studies and evaluate the influence they must have on your aims and requirements. Review and alter the preliminary brief accordingly.

o     This is a critical stage for the client. All problems and new ideas thrown up during the feasibility exercises and site studies will have an influence on the brief. They may well open his eyes to unsuspected possibilities, or cause him to modify the emphasis of his demands or drop some of them altogether.

o     This is the best time to modify or introduce new elements into the brief. What is included now is prompted by the questioning, research and study done by experienced and skilled people – so it will be taken quite seriously by the design team. Also, the design stage proper has not really started. The architect will be keeping an open mind until a comprehensive overall solution begins to emerge.

o     When reviewing the outcome of feasibility and other design studies, do not hesitate to talk to the architect directly.

**2.** Provide all further information requested by the architect.

o     This is the time when the architect will expect the initial brief to be expanded considerably. Knowing that the project is feasible, and with a fair idea of the limits within which the project must be kept, the client can begin the filling-out process. More detailed information should now be added about:

—   More precise accommodation schedule, with critical dimensions.
—   More precise information about space uses, interrelationship of activities and circulation routes.
—   Space heating, lighting and ventilation.
—   All internal requirements, including special environmental factors.
—   Layouts of furniture, fittings and equipment in special rooms and important spaces.
—   Security and welfare provisions.
—   Design data, such as preferred wall or floor finishes.

o     The brief as it grows provides material for design studies on an increasing scale, which in turn can place a demand on the client for more information to be fed into the brief.

**3.** Assist as required in the design studies conducted by the design team.

o     Whilst the brief is developing, the architect and design team will be feeling their way towards a definite design solution. A series of rough sketches will be prepared for discussion amongst themselves and testing against the brief. Repeated attempts will be made until they consider that they have a sketch design which reconciles all requirements of the brief in a balanced way.

## Typical sheet for collecting room data

Name of project:

sheet no:
job no:

Room name                                         minimum area:

Use of room (describe activities)

Relationship to other spaces (grouping, degree of nearness)

Aspect of room

Sound insulation

Finishes (floor, walls, etc.)

Lighting

Heating

Power outlet points

Communication outlets

Ventilation

Equipment

Fixed furniture and use

Free-standing furniture and sizes

Wall fittings

Door sizes

Services: lav basins
        WCs
        sinks

Remarks

o      When seeing the designs, the client will be told of the reasoning behind the tentative solution and the nature of any remaining problems. His acceptance of the interpretation of his requirements, or any criticism or doubts which occur to him, should be expressed. Sometimes his reaction will stir up the architect's thinking about the design scheme and throw it wide open again. This in fact can help to amplify the brief, because the client is drawn more closely into design team operations and has to be more lucid and articulate about aspects of the brief which previously were obscure.

o      Any new contributions from the client, when worked through with the use of more rough sketches, will lead to a synthesis of the incompatibilities. Then alternative schemes will be worked on until a solution emerges which satisfies both parties.

**4.** Initiate and conclude all in-house studies in progress and requested by the architect as the design work proceeds.

o      Carry out in-house research into particular aspects of the brief; search through records, drawings and agreements for the required information. Push forward any work which in-house study teams or departmental groups have in hand in order that conclusions are reached as early as possible in this work stage. Pass all results to the architect.

o      Set up further in-house studies as requested.

o      Obtain the reactions of those who will ultimately use the building to the sketch designs: those of your family, partners, managers, staff and any trade unions involved.

o      Secure from associated organizations such as finance houses or government departments their firm approval in principle to grants or any other financial injections which have been promised.

**5.** Appraise and make decisions on all matters submitted for decision by the architect.

o      From time to time whilst designs develop, the architect will require help in clarifying the client's requirements. Be prepared to visit his office. It can be beneficial for the client or his representative to be present during some of the design sessions. Record all changes agreed to and any new information given during the visits. This is needed to update the brief.

**6.** Consolidate the brief.

o      During this phase, update the brief from time to time to include all additions and changes which are taking place. Make special efforts to record all verbal communications.

### Architect's activities

**1.** Assimilate all information obtained and the client's responses to the feasibility studies and produce diagrammatic analyses; discuss with the design team and bring problems to the client's attention.

o     Study published details and analyses of similar projects.

o     Study the association and arrangement of spaces and circulation routes between them.

o     Call on the client for elaboration of parts of the brief or site documentation to help with studies.

o     Visit recently occupied buildings with the client.

o     Assemble the brief as additional material, changes and decisions are received from the client.

**2.** Try out a detailed planning solution and study the effect which planning and other constraints have on it.

o     Continue with design studies and site development studies.

o     Consult the local planning authority's published development plans and conservation policy documents controlling heights, volumes, elevational treatments, protected features and trees and listed buildings. Record vital requirements in the brief.

o     If necessary, hold informal consultations with the planning officer to help secure formal planning approval.

o     For larger buildings agree a project planning brief with the planning officer.

o     Check that the site survey plans are accurate, and be sure that the developing design sketches will cause no infringement of public footpaths, building lines, road improvement lines, or any access rights, and will not pose any threat to the rights of neighbouring owners. Ask the client to refer to the title deeds of his land and supply extracts affecting the rights of others.

**3.** Prepare several general solutions, discuss with the design team, adjust as necessary and decide on one general approach.

o     During this phase of the design work the client should be shown various possibilities to help weigh priorities and resolve conflicting demands. It could lead to additional material or ideas being offered up which might not otherwise have been included in the brief.

**4.** Prepare the outline scheme drawings and an outline cost plan for the client's consideration.

o     Ideally, the architect will include with the outline sketch designs and outline cost plan a statement of the main elements of the client's brief as received up to this stage. This is done to indicate what the designs are based upon and allows the client to check if there are any omissions or other irregularities.

### General comments

This is an important stage in the development of a brief. It is the time when the client can contribute most to it. He is able to elaborate and add in all the details he wants the architect to take account of. Also, as he responds to questions, appraises sketches, visits buildings and talks to the design team about the brief, a flow of useful information continues for inclusion in the scheme.

Because the design gels at this time, all the outstanding information which the client wishes the architect to have must be thought through, and communicated to him well before this work stage ends.

If the brief has been updated periodically, it will now be approaching a state of completeness.

### 7.3.4  The briefing process (stage D): completing the brief and achieving the scheme design

*Objective*

o    To finalize all information and actions required to render the brief a firm and complete statement.

o    To decide on the quality of the structure and standard of materials to be used.

o    To resolve all the intricacies of conflicting requirements to make way for producing a preferred design solution acceptable to the client and the design team.

o    To finalize scheme design drawings.

o    To obtain statutory approvals.

o    To adjust the cost plan.

o    To produce an approximate estimate of the full project cost.

*Client's activities*

1. Complete the collection of the outstanding items required for the brief, obtain in-house agreement to them and pass to the architect. Attend to all outstanding items such as:

o    Confirming adjustments to room areas, heights and shapes.

o    Determining critical dimensions affecting fittings, equipment or plant to be installed.

o    Providing outstanding data or documents required by the architect concerning the site and its services.

o    Concluding user studies and in-house considerations about space use and space relationships.

o    Ensuring that everyone in your organization has agreed the brief and the additions and amendments made to it.

Ask now if unsure what further information or work the architect needs. However, only you know if an uneasiness exists about previously stated requirements, or whether fresh thought is evolving about something not yet presented to the architect. As this stage of work begins, time for considering options and alternatives is running out, so if you want the architect to consider new ideas, now is the time to tell him. At the end of this stage it becomes necessary to freeze ideas. The brief should be complete.

**2.** Decide on the expected life of the building and any long-term future needs, such as extensions, rearrangements of the internal layouts or upgrading of engineering installations.

o     The performance required of the structure must now be settled in detail. Earlier discussions may have touched on your long-term needs, but you should now review the degree of flexibility the design provides. Be precise about your need for items such as the following:

— Do you wish the main structure to be relatively maintenance-free?
— Have you been able to predict or specify any heavy floor loadings?
— Do you anticipate, even remotely, that some rearrangement of the building interior will be needed in the future?
— Do you anticipate your building being extended in the future?
— Can you foresee needing the installation of additional services in the future? For example, air conditioning may have been dropped from the brief because of its high cost, and you may wish to install it later.

**3.** Confirm any special requirements you might have about the quality and type of finishing materials.

o     If you have first-hand experience of the performance of particular materials, say for flooring in offices and showrooms, or types of doors in garages, you should state a preference.

o     Ask the architect for his ideas about the external finishes. He will at least supply you with a schedule. Get involved for the purpose of thinking about the reasons for the choices. Verify them if you agree.

Some large client organizations can produce performance specifications for the buildings they require, especially if highly specialized (e.g. computer centres or secondary schools). Design data of this kind are invaluable at this stage for clarifying the quality and standards required. Clients who do not have these resources can refer to published briefing and design guides such as those produced by Butterworth Architecture for Libraries, Sports Buildings and Offices.

**4.** Help to remove any remaining obstacles affecting the progress of the project. Attend urgently to any anomalies concerning the interpretation of the brief or preventing the completion of the design.

o     Find out whether the architect is having difficulty with what he may see as conflicts within the brief. If so talk to him about them. Resolve them quickly.

o     Look into the position concerning planning or any listed building consents needed. When the scheme design drawings are finished, a detailed planning application can be made. Be ready to support the architect with this step. It may be desirable to commission special presentation drawings, perspective views or scale models.

o      If an informal approach to the planning authority was made earlier, have discussions been satisfactorily concluded?

**5.** Continue assisting with the design studies being carried out by the design team. Appraise draft scheme designs as developed and modified and approve final scheme design drawings when completed.

o      Appraising the design now involves the client in a wider range of activities. These can include:

— Checking the cost plan and noting the effect that design changes have on it.

— Obtaining observations from potential users of the building.

— Checking that the design conforms with the brief, particularly those detailed sections concerning layouts and specifications of equipment, fittings and fixtures.

— When satisfied with the predicted costs, carrying out a final full review of the design, its layout, areas and detailed requirements, so that approval can confidently be given.

Only after a full scheme design emerges can the preferences, aims and vision of everyone concerned in the project be fully appreciated in terms of the influence they have on the design. It is then that a client may reconsider and alter some of his requirements.

If the client has witnessed the development of the design and been a party to weighing the relative importance of the factors which dictate the form of the building, major changes should not occur at this time. If they do, it will be necessary for the architect to go back to an earlier stage in the designing.

### Architect's activities

**1.** Continue design studies and develop designs to include:

o      Technical performance standards.

o      Requirements of engineering installations.

o      External works and landscaping.

o      All special and abnormal site works.

o      The detailed requirements of planning and other authorities.

These activities lie entirely within the architect's province. The client becomes involved only insofar as he agrees the standard or level of performance proposed. His decisions become part of the client's instructions and are, therefore, part of the brief. If the client is not involved, a statement of the standards and quality of materials proposed should be included in the report which accompanies the scheme design drawings. The client should be advised of variations in the need for special or abnormal requirements of the site, such as special underground works, site drainage or retaining walls. Sometimes, the client is able to claim additional financial assistance for unexpected site development costs. In any case, he should be notified.

**2.** Appraise designs using information about current constructional standards, legislative codes and regulations, design notes, feedback records, technical data concerning constructional materials and methods.

o    When controls or information are discovered which have a significant influence on the design, notes of them should be collected by the architect for inclusion in the client's brief.

**3.** Respond to further additions to the brief in the form of design data, fitting-out information, detailed room layouts, and decisions and modifications of the designs received from the client.

o    Normally the client would supply this information in increments as an addition to his brief. In practice, however, a great deal of the details forwarded to the design team at this time fail to be recorded. It is, therefore, incumbent upon the architect to maintain a method of absorbing this material into his collection of the brief for subsequent agreement by the client.

**4.** After consulting with or taking advice from members of the other professions making up the design team, produce:

o    A set of scheme design drawings.

o    Outline specification notes envisaged for the structural materials and finishes.

o    A developed cost plan.

o    An approximate estimate of cost.

o    Presentation drawings to the standard appropriate to the size and cost of the project.

**5.** On concluding this stage of work, produce a formal report for submission to the client with the scheme design drawings and associated documents.

o    Every care should be taken to ensure that the client understands the drawings and knows the factors embraced in the design.

o    Before seeking approval, check that a thorough appraisal has taken place. Assist if necessary.

### General comments

With the brief settled and the scheme design complete, no further changes should be entertained. This is, of course, a counsel of perfection. In practice small modifications and adjustments are bound to be suggested. Many will be absorbed without causing a major hiccup, but all changes have a penalty. They either add to the professional fees and construction costs, or cause a delay in the project timetable.

## 7.4 The building study visit by client and designers

One of the preliminary steps when beginning to work up an architect's brief is to visit a number of completed buildings along with the architect and other key design staff and consultants. The objective is to present to the client's briefing team and designers some opportunities:
o     To help visualize the forms which certain parts of the projected building's interiors might need to take on.
o     To obtain some clear impressions which can be recalled and discussed when design ideas and details of the brief are being formulated at a later stage.
o     To discuss freely and informally what they see and what they think about it.
o     To give the designers an opportunity to test the client group's reactions to particular characteristics, spatial arrangements and patterns of use displayed by other buildings.

### 7.4.1 Planning the study visit

o     Select a shortlist of buildings which are relatively new and of a similar type and function to the building you require.
o     Invite along all the people who are to be in the group which will represent the client at briefing meetings. This would include the liaison person, and managers and experts most closely involved in the project.
o     Be prepared to make the occasion a study visit for close observation and visual appraisal. A quick look around is not likely to be enough.
o     Stress the importance of mixing freely with the designers, the building users and the building owner's representatives, not just a host!

### 7.4.2 What to do during the study visit

o     Conduct a critical examination of some of the spaces while they are in use.
o     Look carefully at what seems to present an ideal layout or arrangement in spaces such as offices, reception areas, meeting rooms, lounges, display areas and specially designed rooms for accommodating technical activities and specialist equipment.
o     Imagine using the rooms yourself. Put yourself mentally in the position of the people you see using the rooms and equipment.
o     Talk to people working or living in the building to see what they say about it. Ask if they are experiencing any problems, and what they like best about their work areas or living space.

o    If something appears unusual or unworkable, ask questions about it, and mention the point to your architect and designers whilst in the building.

o    It is not the primary purpose of a study visit to look at design or cosmetic features, such as the visual effect of wall treatments or door and window arrangements, from an aesthetic viewpoint. Do not be side-tracked by unusual lighting fittings or exposed service pipework. Impressions to take note of are really more to do with judging the atmosphere or environmental qualities of the individual spaces and the building as a whole.

o    To save time, take photographs of interesting features, layouts or problem areas for reference later.

### 7.4.3  A scenario

The plan shown in Fig 7.2 shows the layout of an optician's shop in the High Street of a very busy town. Through the glass frontage can be seen a 'shop window' display of spectacles and other items being offered and also, close to the doorway, a reception counter. The exterior displays its purpose quite adequately and with dignity, but there is nothing striking about it.

Upon entering, the interior naturally enough presents itself as a reception area and a display area for spectacles. Most prominent are the counter, the receptionists and some seating for people waiting. The transition from the outside, although sudden, brings the visitor to a positive reception point where appointments, enquiries and purchases can be dealt with speedily. It all seemed very efficient!

The visiting client and his architect sat and waited for the optician to show them his surgery and office and the staff room, which were obviously on the first floor. It was whilst sitting waiting that they were able to observe the various activities going on and notice the problems which existed. Comparing notes afterwards revealed:

o    When the shop was quiet, they could clearly overhear a private exchange between a receptionist and an elderly man about a problem with payment.

o    People choosing spectacles had insufficient space and could feel embarrassed being on public view.

o    Too many activities were crowding into this one space:
— Reception.
— General office work and telephoning about appointments and collection of spectacles.
— Simple repair and adjustment of spectacles (in an alcove).
— Waiting.

**Fig 7.2**

Plan of optician's shop

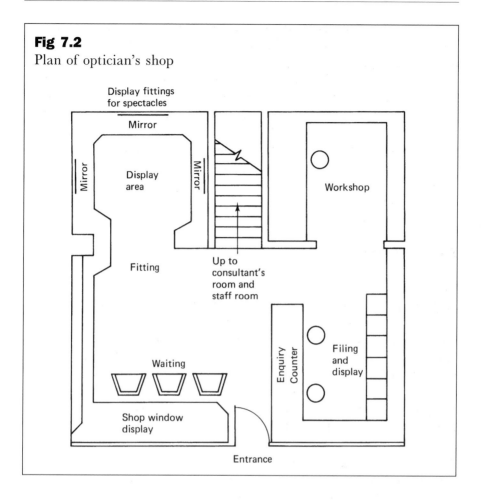

— Fitting of customers and noting down of technical details by an optician.

— General circulation of customers and staff through to the stairs.

— Choosing of new spectacles and receiving advice from an optician.

○ There were many instances of crossing circulation routes causing customers and staff to generally get in each others' way.

○ The final impression obtained, after remaining in the space for about an hour, was that the space was too crowded, noisy and generally uncomfortable for customers choosing spectacles. Some division of functions and activities was desirable. However, the arrangement of the shop gave the staff excellent supervision over the interior – a good security point.

All these reactions point to the need to think through carefully how the plan of a new optician's shop unit could be arranged to meet each anticipated activity.

## 7.5    A list of some typical activities

The list below is a prompt to assist brief writers in the task of thinking out the activities which are to occur in a building and its surrounds.

| Primary activities | Activity groups | Examples |
|---|---|---|
| Industrial | Agricultural | Farming |
| | | Forestry |
| | | Animal husbandry |
| | Manufacturing | Assembling cars |
| | | Making furniture |
| | | Printing |
| Administrative and commercial | Business activities | Office work |
| | | Managing |
| | | Supervising |
| | | Conferring |
| | | Typing |
| | | Computing |
| | | Interviewing |
| | Financing | Accounting |
| | Trading | Buying |
| | | Selling |
| | Protective services | Fire fighting |
| | | Policing |
| Health | Diagnostic | Inspecting |
| Welfare | Welfare | Caring |
| Recreational | Entertainment | Acting |
| | | Singing |
| | Sporting | Swimming |
| | | Darts playing |
| | Leisure activities | Hobbies |
| Worshipping | Church services | Praying |
| | | Hymn singing |
| Learning/information | Research | Experimenting |
| | | Studying |
| | Display | Exhibiting |
| | Information | Data processing |
| | | Telephoning |
| | | Broadcasting |

|  |  |  |
|---|---|---|
|  | Teaching | Explaining |
|  |  | Presenting |
|  |  | Demonstrating |
| Residential | Living | Relaxing |
|  |  | Eating |
|  |  | Sleeping |
|  |  | Viewing TV |
| Common activities | Circulating | Moving |
|  |  | Parking |
|  | Assembly | Spectating |
|  | Resting | Sleeping |
|  |  | Lounging |
|  | Culinary | Cooking |
|  |  | Serving |
|  | Working | Thinking |
|  |  | Handcrafting |
|  |  | Controlling |
|  |  | Managing |
|  | Sanitary | Personal washing |
|  |  | Laundering |
|  | Cleaning | Washing |
|  |  | Vacuuming |
|  | Storage | Stacking |
|  |  | Loading |
|  |  | Filing |
| Outdoor activities |  | Jogging |
|  |  | Gardening |
|  |  | Walking |
|  |  | Travelling |

## 7.6 Reading and interpreting architects' drawings

Everyone knows that architectural or engineering drawings are only a means to an end – the production of a completed building. Sometimes it is hard to remember this when presented with a fine and colourful drawing of your building. Visualizing the volumes and three-dimensional forms which the drawing depicts is a skill which few people possess.

For the inexperienced it is a case of cultivating the art of reading drawings, something that everyone can do with a little practice. Start with a few simple things:

**Fig 7.3**

Reading archirects' drawings: (a) typical site plan, (b) typical floor plan, (c) typical room layout plan

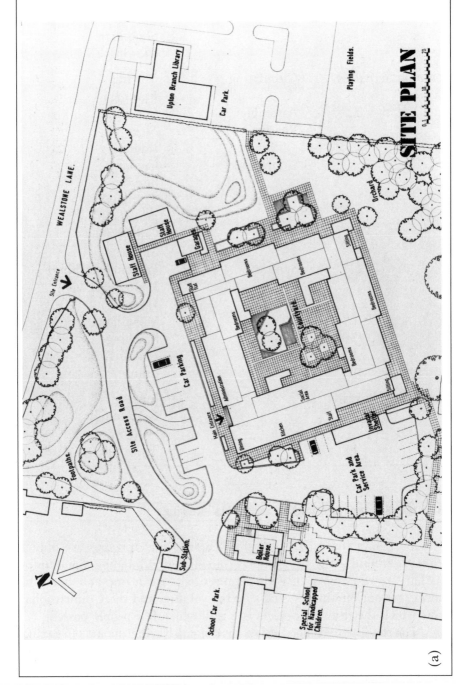

(a)

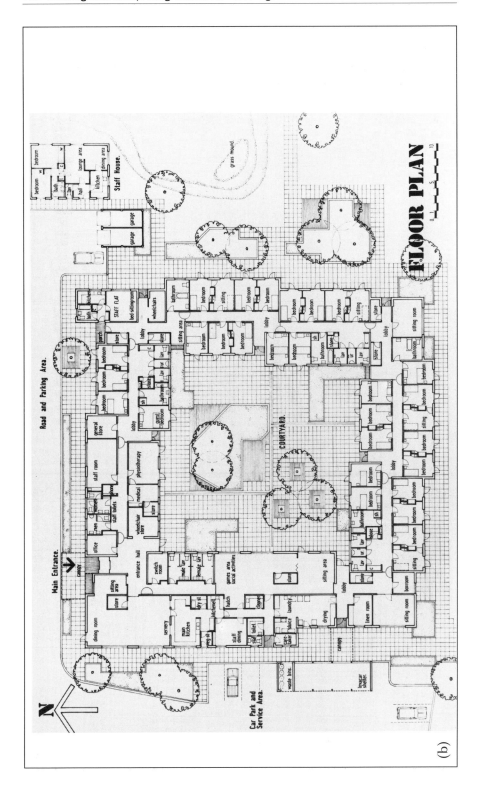

FLOOR PLAN

(b)

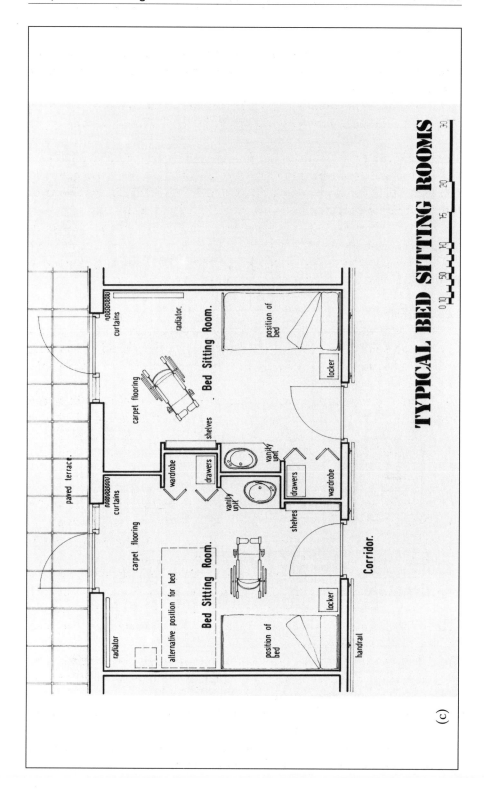

**TYPICAL BED SITTING ROOMS**

(c)

*The plans*

o     Make sure that you are looking at the plans from a viewpoint or location you know. Look first for prominent features such as roadways and other buildings.

o     See how the building is to be set in its surroundings next to adjoining buildings, access roads, car parks, and where the boundaries lie.

o     Find the north point and note which rooms will receive most sun.

o     Look at how the main spaces and rooms are arranged and whether they relate well to one another. Check that the positions of toilets, staircases, storerooms and entrances are satisfactory.

o     Check that you can identify the main routes through the building, such as corridors, lifts and staircases.

o     Identify the symbols which are to be used to represent doors and doorswings, windows, columns, fittings, steps and staircases.

*The elevations*

o     Note if elevations are described by orientation, such as 'elevation to the south', or by names of roads and other flanking features, such as 'elevation to Princes Parkway'. See if you can fit the elevations to the plan.

o     Cross-sections may prove to be harder to understand. They are drawn as though the 'building' is cut vertically along a line which will be found on the plans. This is done to show room heights, clearstorey windows, roof shapes and changes in floor levels, especially on sloping sites.

Avoid some of the common pitfalls by interpreting the drawings together, not in isolation. Some pitfalls to watch for are as follows:

o     If a room does not appear near another on a plan, look to see if it is near vertically on account of a staircase or lift.

o     If a room appears to have no windows, it may have what is referred to as 'clearstorey lighting', where windows are formed high up in the wall and open above a roof. The plan may not show them at all. If lit by rooflights, these would be shown as broken lines on the plan or appear on a roof plan.

o     If elevations appear unrecognizable, it might be because they cannot display all the parts of the building which lie in different planes; one block may be hidden behind the other.

Frequently the client wants to see a realistic view of the building exterior. There are a number of techniques to choose from:

o     *Axonometric and isometric projections,* which are mechanical in construction, can be measured but do not look right.

**Fig 7.4**
Typical perspective drawing (a) and model (b) of the same building

o    *Perspective drawings and sketches*, which are more natural and give a truer impression.

o    *Models*, which would be specially made to show external forms or internal arrangements. They avoid the drawbacks of two-dimensional drawings, but it is still difficult to visualize viewpoints owing to problems of scale.

o    *Computer displays in three dimensions*. Practitioners equipped with computer-generated perspective drawing routines can show reasonably accurate views of a building from almost any preselected viewpoint. Clients might be able to use this facility at an architect's office.

o    *Actual buildings*. There is no substitute for seeing the real thing (even television does not adequately convey the actual spaces, sizes or atmosphere of a building). Visits to buildings already erected are the nearest equivalent and can help you to become more skilful at reading drawings and visualizing what a building will look like.

### After the drawings become understandable to a client

When confident about reading drawings, the client is equipped to interpret them and think about the projected building more as a building than a drawing. It becomes possible to imagine what the physical conditions in a room might be like, such as:

o    The quality of the daylighting, which can be figured out by the size and position of the window and the height of the room.

o    The aspect or amount of sunlight the room will have, by thinking of the position of the sun at various times of the day and how it will affect the room.

o    The prospect, view or outlook from a room, by studying photographs, or taking the drawings to the site and standing 'in' the rooms in question and looking 'out'.

o    The amount of privacy, by looking to see how a room is screened. Look at the doorswing and see if passers by could see directly into the room when the door opens? Or look to see whether passers by have direct views through a window. Would the room be better placed at the end of a corridor or looking out onto a courtyard?

o    The possibility of nuisance from noise in rooms which you know should be quiet, by looking to see if they are segregated from noisy areas and screened from outside noise, such as the noise of motor or railway traffic.

Another possible exercise is to imagine certain well-known activities taking place in the building: trace movements, notice whether rooms and corridors are satisfactorily placed, and check whether fittings and equipment are located correctly. This taxes the imagination, but is really the best way to examine plans of buildings.

For multi-purpose buildings, it is a good idea to set up a working session for some of the client's group and one or two of the designers. Using the plan after the manner of a board game, they analyse complex activities to test whether the building will accommodate them without causing clashes. Routine staff movements and those anticipated for the public can be simulated and monitored to check if they interrelate smoothly during a typical day's or week's activities.

These appraisal methods will either prove the usefulness of the building arrangement or expose conflicts which would affect the building users.

### Types of model

To illustrate the full extent of a project for which full scheme design drawings are available or to portray the architectural quality of a design scheme, choose a *presentation model*. This is a model which attempts to look realistic in form and colour, including all details of the site, surrounding roads, buildings and landscaping. It represents the entire composition envisaged by the design team. Its prime purpose is to help promote the project. It certainly can be made to look quite

**Fig 7.5**
A presentation model

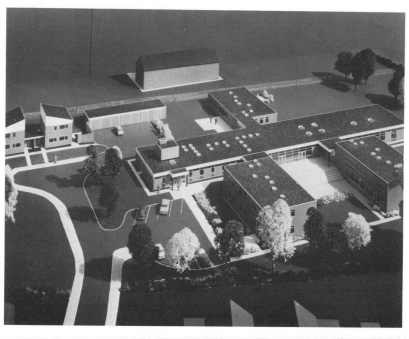

**Fig 7.6**
A block model

impressive. Although costly to produce, it is useful as a support when the approval of other people or organizations is being sought. It can be used for presentation to a management group, a planning authority, or public meeting or exhibition; or as a vehicle to assist with marketing.

To help decide about the general form and heights of the building in its setting early in the design stage, choose a *block model*. This is a very simple model, perhaps produced in balsa wood, portraying the external mass of a building. It may be produced and altered a number of times as the design takes shape. Its prime purpose is to provide a working tool for the architect to use whilst the design is being created. It enables a series of studies to be made of the relationship of its mass with the buildings and natural features surrounding the site.

To study or display the detailed form of part of a building when the overall design of the building is well developed, choose a *detail model*. This is a large-scale model of part of a building to illustrate a particular feature of the design. It is usually made to help visualize rather complex forms or intricate relationships of horizontal and vertical planes. It is a designer's tool to focus attention on important but small parts of the design.

**Fig 7.7**

An interior arrangement model

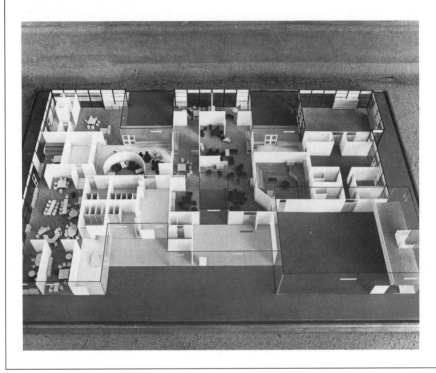

To study or display the form and arrangement of interiors, or to allow interior spaces and layouts of furniture and equipment to be viewed and rearranged if necessary, choose an *interior arrangement model*. This is constructed with some demountable parts to allow the interior to be examined closely. For example, the model of a multi-storey building could have removable roof, walls and floors for this purpose.

To illustrate the relationships of the parts of an initial design and to illustrate new design ideas, choose a *rough* or *'sketch' model*. This conceptual model is fabricated from responsive and flexible materials. It is often symbolic or diagrammatic in character. Its prime purpose is to provide a three-dimensional medium to stimulate reactions, and discussion between the designers and the client, leading to the formulating of further ideas.

### Problems arising with architectural models

There are serious disadvantages which should be kept in mind when deciding whether to have an architectural model made. They undermine the purpose of producing a model in the first place or mislead the onlooker to some degree. Beware of the following.

*Blocking the natural evolution of a design*
Once a model is finished, it tends to be regarded as an object of art in its own right. It tends to take on a meaning which transcends the original purpose of presenting a design scheme – a design which may not in fact be complete or architecturally resolved in the minds of the architects. The model itself can become established in the eyes of the client (and architects) as an artistic achievement in its own right. It is capable of becoming so highly valued as to make any adjustment in its form quite unthinkable. Here the making of a model results in blocking any further development of the design for the building.

*Becoming unduly influenced by the materials used*
Often the materials chosen to construct a model cause misunderstandings about the final appearance of the building. They mislead to some degree by giving an impression of 'solid' sculptural form when this will be seen to be not entirely true when the building is finished.

*Building up a picture from an unrealistic viewpoint*
The natural tendency to look down on the model can leave the onlooker with a clear but unrealistic picture. Models should always be viewed from points which are on a level with the finished ground lines. One easy method is to use an inverted periscope specially produced for the purpose.

*The incorrect use of models to influence or persuade*
Architectural models are an extremely powerful persuasive and influential medium. A client may quickly decide to proceed with a project when he sees his building in model form. Its appeal can be irresistible.

Professional people are usually proud of their work and like to have a presentation model made. There is nothing wrong with this feeling, which the client can also share. However, everyone involved should be aware that should an architectural model be used unscrupulously it is necessary to counter any undue influence.

**Fig 7.8**

Model viewed from an unrealistic viewpoint

**Fig 7.9**

Model viewed from a realistic viewpoint

## 7.7    Decision making for the client during the design phases

It is during the later design stages that all the constraints affecting the design of a building come into effect.

Whether conflicts occur within the brief itself or demands arise from outside considerations, all have to be faced by the person doing the designing – the person sitting in front of a drawing-board. They impinge on the design solution without an observer being aware of it and because some decisions have to be made whilst designing is going on, the client might never realize which constraints are having the greatest influence in shaping the building – not unless the architect mentions them!

As he works, the architect assesses priorities and strikes a balance between the various conflicting demands on the proposed building. Sometimes the problems presented are insuperable and cannot be resolved without a relaxation of one or more constraining requirements. If any arise as a consequence of opposing items contained in the brief, the client will be needed to decide between them. The architect should not have to make these decisions unaided when they are really the responsibility of the client.

Fig 7.10 illustrates the nature of the balancing process which an architect or design team can face on almost any project. When design-ing, all the demands and requirements portrayed here impinge on the architect. They are often in opposition to each other. There is no order of importance or special priority for consideration. Each item needs attention and must be carefully weighed against others to produce a balanced result. Every conflicting demand must be identified and fully resolved if a satisfactory design is to be achieved.

### 7.7.1    Choosing between constraining factors in the brief

Referring to Fig 7.10, it will be seen that some of the subject matter contained in each of the sectors makes rigid demands upon the project design. The character and physical nature of the site is unchangeable, and so are the design standards set by statute for such things as space use, ventilation, daylighting, engineering and construction, fire escape, and facilities for the disabled. There is very likely a cost limit which is to be rigidly applied, and the client's sched-ule of areas could be prescribed by national standards, as in the case of school buildings.

Most flexibility appears to lie in the quantity, quality and type of functional requirements which are chosen by the client, and the amount of finance which is allocated to the project.

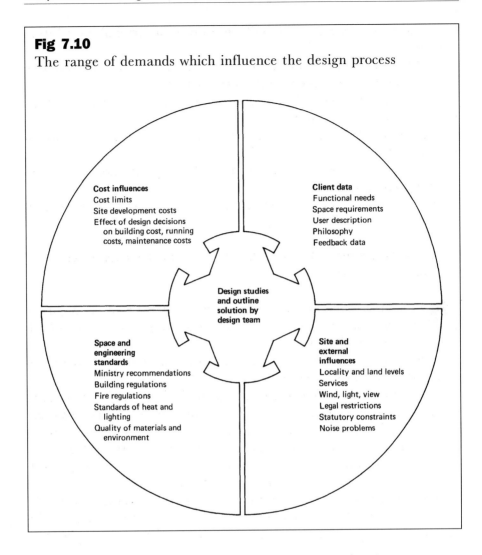

**Fig 7.10**

The range of demands which influence the design process

**Cost influences**
Cost limits
Site development costs
Effect of design decisions
   on building cost, running
   costs, maintenance costs

**Client data**
Functional needs
Space requirements
User description
Philosophy
Feedback data

**Design studies
and outline
solution by
design team**

**Space and
engineering
standards**
Ministry recommendations
Building regulations
Fire regulations
Standards of heat and
   lighting
Quality of materials and
   environment

**Site and
external
influences**
Locality and land levels
Services
Wind, light, view
Legal restrictions
Statutory constraints
Noise problems

Conflicts can arise between any number of competing elements indicated in Fig 7.10, and it is the resolution of these which can make demands on the client to modify the brief.

Skilful design, involving clever exploitation of the site and imaginative arrangement of the plan form, can resolve some of the problems. This is why feasibility and design studies are essential, and why the outcome of these studies can have an influence on the contents of the brief.

You will probably find that pressure naturally arises for you to reduce your requirements for quality matters such as:

o      The extent and widths of circulation routes.

o       Additional space to be 'built in' to provide flexibility for future expansion.

o       Quality of the engineering installations, affecting the standard of the internal environment and control systems.

o       Quality of materials, affecting longevity and money spent on maintenance in the future.

o       Extent of external works, size of car parks and quality of landscaping.

o       Certain spaces or rooms which are desirable but not essential to the functioning of the building.

Also, there could be any number of reasons put forward why you should increase the sums of money allocated to the project.

## 7.7.2   Avoiding some of the late adjustments to the brief during the scheme design phase

Having to make numerous late adjustments to the brief might be avoided if a rigorous stand is taken when briefing first begins. Eliminate some of the changes by:

o       Discussing possible environmental standards and the quality of materials at an early meeting with the architect.

o       Having a cost study prepared by a building economist or quantity surveyor as soon as possible after the initial brief has been prepared.

o       Ensuring that a cost plan is produced as soon as the first sketches are produced at outline scheme stage (RIBA Plan of Work, stage C).

o       Carefully updating the cost plan from time to time during development of the brief and continuation of the design.

Do not overlook the potential which exists in seeking advice about the ultimate cost of the project when only an initial brief is available. The analytical possibilities for appraising the brief and forecasting the costs involved are quite extensive.

Comparative studies of the final construction costs of other similar completed buildings can be made which will indicate whether the total area of the accommodation asked for in the initial brief is too great in proportion to the other services and installations which are normally required.

Ask at the earliest meeting with the architect whether cost planning procedures are appropriate to your project and how to obtain them.

# The form and composition of the brief

*(handwritten: all pages)*

**Here a comprehensive checklist is given which covers the contents of an ideal final brief**

o      An outline list for use as a prompt when writing down a first statement of need.

o      An expanded list of items which will assist you as brief writer to identify and record the facts and requirements which are particular to your building project.

When first setting down an initial brief, or developing it into a full and detailed statement, there are three main groups of information to be worked on. These groups are set out below with an indication of what would normally be included in them.

*1. Purpose and policy*
A description of the purpose of the project and the client's policy about how much money and time to allocate to it, including such things as:

o      Basic purpose and overall function.

o      Scope and content of the project.

o      Demand, expressed in terms of recorded inadequacies in an existing building.

o      Client's resources, his own advisers and any in-house professional skills which can be called on.

o      Known limitations of such things as overall permissible building area, construction cost, time deadlines, mandatory standards and dimensions, or any priorities such as phasing of parts of the project.

*2. Operational factors*

A description of the desired activities and functions of the project and the methods by which the completed project is to be run, including such things as:

○      Activities to be accommodated.

○      Who is to use the building.

○      Number and types of staff, employees and regular users and visitors.

○      How the activities will be run and organized to relate to one another; for example the manufacturing, administration and management operations, an educational curriculum, or the timetabling of jointly used spaces.

○      Communications systems required to run the proposed activities and organization.

*3. Design requirements*

The known and anticipated physical needs for the internal environment and the surrounds of the building, down to the smallest conceivable detail:

○      Internal and external environment, in terms of the conditions and effect aimed at.

○      Siting and external requirements.

○      Schedule of accommodation, space requirements and specific groupings.

○      Layout and zoning, including relationships between spaces.

○      Movements of pedestrian and vehicular traffic.

○      Equipment, plant, fittings and fixtures.

○      Requirements for services and engineering installations, and the standards and controls required.

○      Any preferred constructional standards.

○      All cost implications; the cost plan and approximate estimates of cost, including all revisions and updates.

This outline could be used as a prompt when writing down your first statement of need. At this stage it is not possible to produce an accurate and succinct statement which represents the complete idea of what is wanted. It will, however, set in motion an evolutionary process which leads naturally to producing a real working brief – something the architect can confidently respond to.

After preliminary meetings with the architect, a more complete version of the brief will be needed and the first statement will have to be filled out.

The following checklist is offered to assist with the production of the various stages of the brief as it develops. All the items should be methodically reviewed from time to time to be sure all relevant subject matter is being worked on.

## 8.1    The form and composition of the brief – a checklist

Using the lists which follow, set down your requirements for each of the items which apply to your project. Collect your ideas first in the form of notes grouped in separate sections or on separate sheets of paper. Start at any point in the checklist and continue in any order which suits you.

Try to state requirements without envisaging a form which you think might suit you. Think more of the circumstances which must prevail rather than a predetermined form. Not: 'My office should be 12 metres square and look just like the Director's.' Rather 'My work involves three identifiable activities, quiet research, consultation with groups of up to eight people, and the usual hurly burly of dealing with sudden individual contacts by telephone or by staff looking in.'

Indicate how firm your requirements are as you write. Any uncertain requirements, and those items which temporarily puzzle you, can then be picked up at meetings with the architect.

The checklist represents the contents of a final brief. After writing an initial outline brief, you should expect to use the list several times until a final brief is completed.

Normally, one or more intermediate briefs will be compiled as the client's needs become clearer and sketch designs emerge. Each brief is more detailed and explicit than the last, a process which avoids the obscuring of the main aims and policy matters with excessive detail at the early stages.

### 8.1.1    Part 1: Purpose and policy

*Basic purpose and overall function*
o    Basic purpose and function of the project:
—    Project title, address, postcode and map reference.
—    Outline kind of project in general terms.
—    State whether project is an extension, a new 'green field' or town infill scheme, or a refitting or refurbishing scheme.
—    Main reasons for project: replacement, renewal of structure, expansion?
o    Client's organization:
—    Diagram showing hierarchy and roles, managerial responsibilities.
o    Project organization:
—    Name of client's liaison officer (for all formal communication with the architect and design team members).
—    Names of participating staff and any related groups.

— Administrative and control procedures.
— Contractual methods.
— Site supervision methods.

### *Historical background and present position*

o       All activities and incidents to date:
— Past events and decisions.
— Development approvals received or lapsed.
— Previous studies, surveys, appraisals and investigations.
o       Current position:
— Currently running studies.
— Any existing ongoing commissions or contracts and consultant or contractor involved.
— Problems highlighted.
— Planning applications awaiting decision.
— Uncertainties remaining about past incidents, the results of any studies or current activities.

### *Aims*

o       Define prime objectives:
— Operational needs.
— Social and cultural.
— Energy and maintenance.
— Value for money.
— Time-scale.
o       Philosophy affecting the way the project is to be used:
— How the occupier relates to the environment, impressions he should have.
o       Intended values and image to be portrayed:
— Impact on onlookers, visitors, users.
— First impressions and long-term opinion to be transmitted.
— Atmosphere and the intrinsic qualities aimed at.
o       Insight for the future, concerning the client and his organization, business or family:
— A broad attempt at future changes which could come along, evolutionary events which could dictate enlargement or shrinkage of the project.
o       Degree of flexibility desired for future changes:
— Any options for reorganization, rearrangement and refitting in the future.
— A close fit of the space requirements may not be wise.

## Scope and content of the project

o    Size, overall area:
—    Initially assess size or area by referring to similar-type buildings.
—    Some projects derive from a square metre basis multiplied by numbers of users.
o    Minimum usable area:
—    Sometimes the net working area can be ascertained; in schools the areas devoted to teaching, in offices the working areas excluding corridors and ancillary spaces.
o    Description of constituent parts:
—    List each separate department, suite, section and unit with differing functions.
o    Relationships and specific groupings:
—    Indicate how departments and suites link or relate together.
—    Any self-contained or independent suites?
o    The site and its surrounds:
—    Indicate location, extent, orientation, boundaries and access points on a site plan or ordnance sheet.
—    State ownership and occupancy rights, whether owner, purchaser or tenant.
—    Have legal adviser summarize all restrictions, easements and conditions from deeds or conveyance.
—    Include copies of all relevant legal documents.
—    Describe characteristics, particularly features which should be retained, e.g. transport facilities, landscape and trees, water-courses, archaeology.
o    Extent of site works:
—    Any land to remain undeveloped, unchanged.
—    Any related works to be situated outside the site boundaries: access roads, service mains, outfall drains.
o    Things to be avoided.

## Defined demand

o    Recorded inadequacies in an existing building:
—    Reported faults, e.g. available spaces badly arranged or too small, aged and impossible to upgrade, overcrowded, poor-quality environment.
o    Results of user surveys:
—    Summarize conclusions from report/s.
—    Attach survey report/s.
o    Findings of postmortem appraisals of other buildings:
—    Collect comments, feedback items and conclusions.
—    Include experiences of occupying other buildings (good and bad).

### Client's resources

o     List own advisers upon whom the architect may call:
—     Retained financial, legal and technical advisers and managerial consultants.
—     State authority needed by the architect before consulting one of them.
o     Name any in-house professional staff and specify special skills which you or your colleagues may possess:
—     List staff and area of expertise and how to communicate with them.
—     State any authority needed before approaching individual staff concerned.


### Known limitations

o     State any overall permissible building area imposed from any source:
—     State limits to overall areas if any imposed by government or grant-aid bodies.
o     Express any limits to the ultimate construction cost:
—     Declare any rigid cost limit.
o     Define any rigid time deadlines.
—     Consider time limits and specify priorities, such as phasing of parts of the project.
—     Define zones, departments, suites and ideal priorities.
—     Add agreed priorities to project timetable.
o     Any mandatory standards and dimensions:
—     Name guidebooks and all individual references to standards wherever possible.
—     Quote overall sizes of large items of key equipment, gantries, plant, and special vehicles and transporters.
—     Include perimeter areas, operating distances and tolerances.
—     Check if any government maximum room areas are recommendations or strict limits.
o     Any set demands for reducing maintenance costs or running costs:
—     If you have a policy refer to it, otherwise investigate what is possible with the architect and add to the brief later.
—     If very sensitive about security or being overlooked by workmen, consider a low-maintenance exterior.
o     Define the quality of the structure, materials to be used or the engineering installations:
—     If you have a policy refer to it, otherwise investigate what is possible with the architect and add to the brief later.

o      Indicate the client's financial resources for the project:
—   Loans or capital contributions from sponsors.
—   Availability of finance, approval of machinery and timing.
—   Any input from grants or subsidies.
—   Are qualifying elements for a grant bound up in the physical condition or design of the building?
o      State any limits of capital costs (or costs-in-use):
—   Cost target.
—   Acceptable cost variations.
—   Contingency allowances for risk.
—   Penalties for late completion to be imposed?
—   Calculate budget on predicted costs, including professional fees.
o      Work out a design and construction programme:
—   Set target dates for main stages of work, for example:
    1. Agreement of initial brief.
    2. Set working meeting dates.
    3. Agreement of scheme design.
    4. Agreement of final brief.
    5. Completion of working drawings.
    6. Tender receipt date.
    7. Completion of negotiated tender.
    8. Availability of site or building.
    9. Start of site operations.
   10. Completion date.
   11. Commissioning period.
   12. Date of occupation.

### Communications systems

o      Describe the communication systems required to run the activities and organization to be accommodated, including goods supply systems, production process control and office routines. Consider any need for:
—   Tannoy, closed-circuit TV.
—   Satellite transmitters/receivers.
—   Computer data and TV cable links.
—   Automation.
o      Describe telecommunications requirements:
—   Central equipment and switchgear.
—   Instruments, telex equipment.
—   Degree of flexibility.
—   Computer modems.

### 8.1.2    Part 2: Operational factors

*Activities to be accommodated*

o      Define all activities to be accommodated and group them in the
following way:
— List the main overall activity groups (or zones of activity) which
have already been defined in terms of departments, suites,
sections or units with particular functions.
— Using these overall activity groups as headings, define and write
down the primary activities which contribute directly to each
overall activity.
— Add on the secondary or supporting activities which serve each
overall activity (indicate the secondary status in every instance).
— List separately the secondary or supporting activities which serve
the building as a whole, such as sanitary and hygiene, cleaning,
safety and maintenance of plant and installations.
— Indicate within the overall activity groups any occasional activities which may be envisaged.

There is a hierarchy of activities mentioned here. In the case of an
activity like 'conferring' or 'formal meeting' you might obtain a result
like:

> *Conferring (overall activity):*
> Formal meeting of directors.
> Viewing films or video presentations.
> Viewing exhibits, drawings, photographs, etc.
> Staff seminars, presentations.
> Taking occasional refreshments (primary activities).
> Accommodate coats, umbrellas and briefcases.
> Opportunity for individual telephoning (secondary activities).
> Provision for dining/hospitality (occasional activity).

o      Describe the working methods of individuals:
— Indicate alongside each activity the contributory techniques and
methods which are important to you or the people involved.
— Indicate the duration and frequency of each activity.
— In factories, study the spatial movements of people and vehicles,
and the operating requirements for the control, monitoring and
maintenance of manufacturing machinery.
— In homes, indicate how you like to use your audiovisual equipment, whether it is operated from a central point or dispersed.
o      This exercise greatly influences the size, layout and equipping
of spaces. For example:
— An executive who has a variety of files and papers currently in

use may prefer to spread them out on a large table top. He likes the visual reminder this gives him and the ease with which he can move from one subject to another. How many 'stacks' does he need, and how are they usually arranged?

— A writer or researcher may prefer to have a number of books, papers and notes spread out in a particular way for frequent reference. What is his working arrangement?

— Mechanics working continually and rapidly on a fleet of vehicles have a routine to follow. How often do they need to work on the undersides of vehicles? What equipment is used most frequently?

o    Describe the flow of any industrial or manufacturing process and the operating sequences of major equipment and plant:

— Indicate diagrammatically the form which the material production lines will take.

— Illustrate each step in the flow of the materials and units being fabricated as they pass through the production sequences.

o    Describe the flow of tasks through an office organization:

— Indicate diagrammatically the normal route which subject matter (documents or electronic data) takes through an office organization and illustrate each step in the work process.

o    Describe any preferred sequential flow of people through a building or an activity zone:

— Changing rooms, display areas, galleries, airport or bus depot reception areas, showrooms, foyers, self-service counters, etc.

o    Work out the relationships between each of the main activities:

— Establish the connections which must exist if the occupants are to relate happily, comfortably and conveniently to each other.

— Establish the connections which are necessary to ensure that an occupying organization will function efficiently.

— Note down how near each activity and occupant need to be to one another:
1. In same space, within earshot.
2. Adjacent, en suite.
3. Close, within (say) 10 metres.
4. Distance immaterial, must be on same floor or in same block.

— Indicate how often communication between people, records and goods takes place:
1. Very frequently.
2. More than five times per day.
3. Less than three times per day.
4. Three times or less a week.
5. Infrequently.

To deal properly with this part of the brief involves finding out how people move about to do their tasks. For large projects, you can build up a diagram such as that in Fig 8.1, normally referred to as an inter-action or relationship matrix. For small projects, sketch out the ideal relationship of spaces or activities you would like to see, regardless of whether it results in a recognizable or rational shape. But always think of the activity being carried out and how it relates to others.

o      State if there are any restrictions on the positioning of activities:
—      State if there are activities which cannot be placed on upper floors.
—      Note down those activities and spaces which must open directly to the outside.
—      Are there any limitations to the use of lifts, staircases and ramps?
o      Describe the circulation factors governing layouts and the use of upper floors:
—      Indicate desirable routes and acceptable distances between:
       1. Zones of activity.
       2. Particular spaces which are important to you.
       3. The various processes which are to take place in the building.
These exercises can become easier if diagrams are produced, however rough they might be. The result could be in the form of a 'bubble' diagram similar to that shown in Fig 8.2.
o      Consider space needed for movement in and around equipment or furniture arrangements in special rooms:
—      Indicate if you know of additional space requirements to accom-modate movements in connection with the conduct of special or complex activities.
An architect may not be able to anticipate the range of movement associated with particular activities or combinations of activities when carried out in one space. Only the client may know. The need for any additional movement space should be stated early in the preparation of the brief, well before room layouts are studied. For example, when a team of people use the same office area, extra movement space could be required; an examination of the way in which the work is handled will show where individuals should sit in order to carry out their tasks, and move easily to filing, storage and other pieces of equipment. Another example is the amount of space required around a bath for nurses when bathing a patient; possibly there needs to be a sunken well in the floor to reduce the amount of bending for the nurse.
o      Consider access for pedestrian and vehicular traffic:
—      State number required, any segregation at entrances, special widths, security controls and supervision, automatic door opening, remote operation with phone link, or draught-free provision.

## Fig 8.1

Matrix illustrating journeys between rooms by people working in a typical existing operating theatre suite. This can be used to decide what modifications are needed to reduce movement to a minimum and to combine the units in the most satisfactory way from all known points of view. (From *The Architects' Journal*, 17 June 1964, p. 1375.)

Total Journeys

| 117 | 1 | Sisters' changing room |
| 171 | 2 | Nurses' changing room |
| 717 | 3 | Surgeons' rest room |
| 399 | 4 | Surgeons' changing room |
| 46 | 5 | Superintendent's room |
| 24 | 6 | Medical store |
| 395 | 7 | Small theatre |
| 376 | 8 | Anaesthetic room no 1 |
| 711 | 9 | Theatre room no 1 |
| 528 | 10 | Sink room |
| 488 | 11 | Sterilising room |
| 677 | 12 | Scrub up room |
| 1115 | 13 | Ante-space and nurses' station |
| 711 | 14 | Theatre room no 2 |
| 376 | 15 | Anaesthetic room no 2 |
| 395 | 16 | Emergency theatre |
| 254 | 17 | Workroom and clean supply |
| 146 | 18 | Sterile supply room |
| 249 | 19 | Male staff changing room |
| 546 | 20 | Nurses' station |
| 305 | 21 | The entrance |

## Fig 8.2

Bubble diagram used as a first step for generating actual plan layout of a building

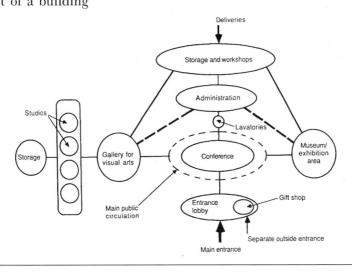

○     Are any lifts, hoists or escalators required?

—     Indicate preferences and any special characteristics you know of.

○     Are there special requirements concerning staircases and ramps?

—     Any preferred gradients?

—     Any points where changes of floor level are not acceptable?

### Who is to use the building

○     Describe generally the groups or individuals who are to occupy and use the building:

—     Describe type, age, sex and numbers of users, residents or visitors, e.g. pupils, boys and girls of 11 years to 16 years of age, or general visiting public, 100 to 175 per day.

—     Consider status in organization, the special needs of any disabled users or users with different skills and backgrounds where this might affect the character or quality of their accommodation.

○     Describe numbers and types of staff employees, regular users and visitors:

—     List staff categories, including managers and all residents and visitors.

○     State time and frequency of occupation:

—     Routine of members of a household.

—     Office and factory working hours, any limits to overtime or shift working.

—     Daily routine and timetable for residents of a hostel.

—     School or college hours, and timetable.

—     Times for after-hours cleaning and maintenance work.

This information will be readily available for projects required by local authorities. In police or fire stations, the numbers of operational officers, personnel and civilian staff will already be known. In the case of old-persons' homes or hostels, details of the staff and all residents to be cared for will be readily available. Most large organizations will have a staff establishment list which could be included in the brief.

### How activities are to be run and organized to relate to one another

○     Describe method of managing the building, its occupants, processes and daily routine:

—     Reception arrangements.

—     Managerial routines, involving warden, supervisor, chief officer, office manager and subordinates.

—     Organization's management procedures for departments, sections and groups with lines of command clearly shown.

—     First-aid arrangements and facilities.

—     Computerized routines for control of the environment.

○   — Janitor and cleaning.
○   Illustrate management structure (with a diagram):
    — This will indicate to the architect how the various parts of the
      organization are coordinated and how decisions are taken.
○   Consider security, controlled areas and supervision:
    — Control on access by strangers, time clocks for staff.
    — High-security suites.
    — Card-operated door locks.
    — Security and surveillance methods.
    — Local fire detectors, alarms and fire-fighting equipment within
      the organization.

### Items to be housed

○   Describe all items to be housed, whether permanent or
transient; quote dimensions, weights and characteristics:
    — Static items, such as machinery, workbenches and equipment.
    — Loose and heavy items of furniture, such as bookracks, billiard
      tables and safes.
    — Mobile items, such as vehicles, cranes, gantries and animals.
    — Transitory items, such as raw materials, manufactured products,
      waste products and any by-products for which space may have to
      be found.

### Storage requirements

○   Determine the extent of storage required by considering the
needs of particular centres of activity, for example:
    — In homes and hostels:
      1. Storage units for food and clothes.
      2. Space for general items not in everyday use (such as film and
      slide projectors).
      3. Space for items which are related to dining, cooking, dressing,
      bathing, sleeping and outdoor activities.
    — In office suites storage for items such as:
      1. Personal effects, coats, handbags.
      2. Paper, forms, instruments, books, items needed near
      workspace.
      3. General stationery storage.
      4. Plan filing cabinets.
      5. Replacement items for equipment.
      6. Dead file store.
      7. Computer data disks.
    — Whatever building you require, look at the activities which go on

in your own or another building. This will prompt you to decide
what storage space is desirable.

o    Compile a list of storage requirements; indicate generally the
items to be stored:

—    Study each activity area separately and enlist the help of family,
     colleagues or staff to highlight particular needs and record them.

If this information is noted down in a sketchy fashion early in the briefing process, it alerts the designers to what is needed well before the
preliminary designs firm-up. It is often impossible to squeeze in
adequate storage space during the later design stages. As the brief is
developed, these notes can be filled out and details of quantities,
dimensions and illustrations added.

### Degree of flexibility required

o    Consider whether any flexibility of layout, arrangement and
overall size is desirable:

—    Is it likely that more people will need to be accommodated?
—    Can you imagine some activities altering?
—    Should parts of the interior be capable of rearrangement?
—    Is it likely that services installations could be improved or added
     to in the future?

o    State degree of flexibility required:

—    Percentage increase of people, equipment or throughput of work.
—    State activity zones where changes are not foreseen at all.
—    State type of additional services or services likely to alter in the
     future.

In the life of a building, changes are inevitable. Ideally, they should be
anticipated by the brief. It requires insight and some imagination to
forecast probable changes, but if at all possible a forecast should be
attempted.

Deciding about the degree of flexibility to build into a project is
a most difficult assignment, both for the client and architect. However,
the following points might prove helpful.

It is unwise to tailor a building too closely to the areas and activities envisaged when producing a brief. It leaves the building so tightly
constrained that stress is felt throughout the building when an increase
in demand occurs.

It has been said that if a building is built to last and operate
over a long period of time, a loose-fitting shell is essential. This is good
in theory, but generous overprovision of floor area, when applied
throughout the building, can prove wasteful. It is better to provide
latitude to the spaces which are known to be susceptible to change, or
the areas which accommodate the activities most difficult to define.

### Design requirements

Up to this point the client has been encouraged to use a particular technique when following the first two parts of this checklist. This involves:

○    Expressing ideas, aims and objectives.

○    Setting down facts and assessments about the users.

○    Describing the circumstances which must prevail in the building.

○    Translating all spacial requirements into activities.

○    Thinking of the objects to be housed rather than the building itself.

Using this technique will have meant suppressing all preferences for the shapes or sizes of things, or for the areas and dimensions of rooms – or even the ultimate form which the building might adopt.

Part 3 of the checklist is different. It is a prompt and an outline against which both client and architect can record everything concerning the physical nature of the project. The part of the brief compiled using this part of the checklist will include data and decisions which will have arisen in a number of ways:

○    Out of the work the client has already done with Parts 1 and 2 of this checklist.

○    From decisions made at meetings between the client and architect or design team.

○    From decisions made following completion of feasibility studies, site studies and user surveys.

○    From appraisals of preliminary design drawings.

○    From briefing material produced in the past for other similar buildings.

○    From various outside sources.

As facts, decisions and hard data gradually build up during development of the brief and initial designs, they can form a collection based on Part 3 of the checklist. Contributions may come to hand during the initial briefing stage, whilst work is being done on Parts 1 and 2 of the checklist. If this happens, they should be collected under the headings of Part 3 of the checklist.

Items placed in the collection will remain fluid until the project is well into the scheme design stage – items being varied in response to changing ideas and the clearer views of everyone concerned. For example, accommodation schedules and performance requirements specified by external bodies, such as national or regional government departments or funding organizations, would be included in the collection as soon as the information comes to hand. This ensures that these standards, which are often advisory and sometimes mandatory, can be readily produced as a yardstick for comparison with the client's own preferences and the results of the sketch designs. Sometimes alternative schedules of accommodation are generated following computer analyses of space needs and the timetabling of its use. It can be held in the collection until a final choice is made.

When using the Part 3 checklist, you will find that it provides:

o    A reliable way of collecting and organizing a large variety of facts and information as they come to hand.

o    A convenient way of recording decisions as they are made, reviewed and revised.

o    A practical way of producing an element of the brief which provides the architect with a sound basis for all stages of the design work.

### 8.1.3    Part 3: Design requirements

*Schedule of accommodation, space requirements and specific groupings*

o    Draw up accommodation schedule with room areas:
—    List halls, rooms and spaces for which activities have already been determined.
—    Include spaces which it is known may not be fully enclosed or partitioned off.
—    State floor area of each room or space (measured within internal faces of enclosed walls).
—    Include recommended schedule of rooms with areas received from others (for comparison purpose).

o    State any critical dimensions – volumes, areas, lengths, widths or heights:
—    Operating distances for machinery, production techniques, turncircle of special vehicles, critical dimensions of openings, garage doors, bridge heights, headroom for special activities and objects.
—    Include all dimensions which you know about.

*Grouping, zoning and layouts*

o    Indicate spaces which must function as a unit or group:
—    Rooms which need to be close together to function properly – a suite.
—    Suites of rooms which need to be close together to function properly – a zone or department.
—    Indicate if certain suites of rooms, or departments, are preferred to be located on differing floor levels or in separate, defined blocks and state reasons.

o     Show key relationships and links between departments, zones, suites or rooms and spaces:
—   Describe or prepare diagrams or schedules.
—   State any limits to travel distances between spaces.
o     Set out intricate patterns of relationships where these occur:
—   Produce a 'bubble' diagram, arrangement chart or relationship matrix.

### Movements of people, goods, mobile equipment and animals

o     Describe patterns of movement.
o     Indicate intensity and frequency of traffic.
o     Number of access points, any segregation?
o     Any restrictions to private or secure suites?
o     Exits and escape routes.
o     Waiting areas.
o     Any moving pavements.

### External requirements and site layout

o     Consider all factors relating to the surroundings which may affect the site; layout, unwanted shadows, overlooking properties and noisy motorways.
o     Describe and list any off-site works, drainage, supply services, pavement crossings or footpath links to adjoining buildings.
o     Patios, terraces and special paved surfaces.
o     Recreation requirements, games and play areas, including related storage.
o     Access for vehicles, cyclists and pedestrians.
o     Restriction for animals; ditches, electrified barriers, cattle grids?
o     Barriers, fencing and gates.
o     Areas to be screened.
o     Landscaping and planting.
o     Areas to be left in a virgin state.
o     Recontouring, formation of pools, land drainage, protection against flooding.
o     External furnishings, seats, litter bins, bollards and notice-boards.
o     Outside lighting, including display lighting or for illuminating the building itself.
o     Decorative features and artworks.
o     Direction signs.
o     Garaging, car ports and car parking.
o     Structures for waste disposal, fuel storage, drainage pumps.
o     Underground tanks or storage space.

## Movements of vehicular traffic
o    Vehicle routes and turning circles.
o    Access for emergency services – fire, ambulance and police.
o    Any restricted areas for access or parking?
o    Any traffic signalling?

## Condition and quality of internal environment
Describe occupancy conditions, amenities and effects:
o    Indicate acceptable temperature bands and humidity levels and any special conditions for activities or materials to be housed.
o    Indicate preferred types of lighting; quality of daylighting, artificial lighting, and any sun control, shading or tinting of glass.
o    Internal landscaping.
o    Indicate acoustic requirements of rooms and halls, whether for music, speech or a combination of both.
o    Indicate where sound insulation is needed and the degree of sound reduction required between rooms.
o    Describe the degree and character of privacy, whether light or complete screening, or whether a private or secondary access route is needed.

## Requirements for engineering installations
State the standards and controls required for:
o    *Heating and cooling:*
  —   Thermal factors, temperature limits, heating or cooling season, and any changes between zones of the building.
o    *Lighting:*
  —   Natural and artificial lighting levels.
  —   Emergency lighting, type and extent, batteries.
  —   Display lighting.
o    *Ventilation:*
  —   Describe prescribed or desirable air changes.
  —   Indicate preferences for opening lights.
o    *Energy demands:*
  —   State type of fuel and means of storage.
  —   Specify standby requirements and preferred standby systems.
  —   Consider solar energy as a possibility and state requirements.
o    *Power requirements:*
  —   Overall loading.
  —   Any on-site transformer equipment and housing.
  —   Any restrictions on fuel storage.

### *Any preferred constructional or architectural standards affecting the fabric of the building*

○      Factors relating to preferred form, scale, texture, colour, proportion and architectural style (if any):

—    Architectural features of previous building, perhaps destroyed by fire, which are to be reproduced as part of the project.

—    Records of architectural elements to be preserved as part of the project.

—    Planning brief set as an architectural design constraint by the local planning authority.

—    Client's own architectural requirements (if any).

—    Specify graphic design and logo if any.

○      Factors affecting materials to be used:

—    Quote requirements for floor or wall finishes in particular spaces where this is important.

—    If an extensive list is to be given, produce a room-by-room schedule.

○      Quote all known superimposed loads:

—    Research and state weights of heavy loads to be carried on upper floors, e.g. heavy machinery, safes, library book stacks and shelving.

—    State acceptable limits of structural deformation.

○      Research degree of exposure of building and acceptable wind loads:

—    Specify the required wind loading on the whole structure or on particular parts.

○      Study and record legislative requirements affecting the building:

—    Means of fire escape, prescribed widths of corridors and staircases, frequency and enclosure of staircases.

—    Fire protection of structure, fire divisions and enclosure of structural materials.

—    Requirements for prevention of spread of flame.

—    On-site fire-fighting equipment and installations.

—    Distances from boundaries.

○      Describe degree of protection required against contamination:

—    Quote ventilation needs and control systems.

—    Specify humidity requirements and controls.

—    Select preferred security systems, alarms, telecom links, closed circuit TV, security screens, doors and locks.

### *Fittings, fixtures, equipment and loose furniture*

○      Draw up a schedule of the fittings, equipment and loose furniture to be accommodated:

—   Select generally the type and quality of fittings and furniture to be accommodated, so that they are easily coordinated and inter-changeable in future rearrangements of the interior.

—   Prepare a room-by-room schedule of the minimum number of items needed in each location.

—   For some rooms, produce diagrams to show preferred relation-ships of equipment, fixtures, fittings and loose furniture.

It is inadvisable to conceive a brief without identifying the furnishing needs. It is an integral part of the concept and demands analysis in great detail. Each activity or space should be analysed individually to assess the type and arrangement of fixed and moveable furniture needed to meet every functional need. Take care to select only the minimum amount of furniture necessary to enable each space in the building to operate fully. Remember that some individual items can be designed or selected to satisfy more than one function.

### Cost implications of the building project (excluding site acquisition costs)

o      Include a statement of the budget which is being worked to and break it down into the following main elements:

—   *Nett cost.* The cost of the building itself, a figure prescribed by using a cost yardstick set either by an outside organization or assessed from detailed knowledge of costs of similar buildings.

—   *Additional costs.* All costs of work external to the building affect-ing the site and surrounds to the building.

—   *Abnormal costs.* Unusual work needed to allow the chosen site to be developed: special constructional work to combat sharply falling ground levels, filled ground, effects of mining subsidence, subterranean features such as culverts, old foundations, etc.

—   *Professional fees.* An assessment of the fees and expenses charge-able by each of the consultants to be engaged on the project.

—   *Taxes and supervisory costs.* Charges for planning and building regulation submissions, legal costs for drawing up the building contract, and salaries of any clerk of works or site engineer to be retained by the client.

o      Provide a contingency reserve fund:

—   Ideally, a sum should be set aside from the budget amount declared by the client to meet additional costs arising from any unforeseen problems.

—   Predict the value of the increased costs of labour and materials which will result from the effects of inflation, and decide how to meet them.

○    Include a cost plan of how the budget will be allocated to various parts of the building, and include all revisions and updates:

— Use cost planning techniques as a tool to ensure that the proposed form of the buildings, its constructional method and the materials to be used can be produced for the budgeted project cost.

# Some commonly used techniques and aids to briefing

**Choosing a strategy for working which is appropriate to the client's experience and the size and complexity of the project**

In this section different strategies are offered to serve:
o     A first-time client.
o     A regular or repeat client.
o     An expert and experienced client.
o     A combination of clients who are working jointly on a project;
and also different kinds of buildings such as:
o     A very high quality building.
o     Adaptation or refitting of an existing building.
o     A jointly used building for more than one client.
o     A very large building which is to be built in a number of separate stages.
Also some details are given about the use of checklists, questionnaires, cost planning, computer aids, design sessions and briefing conferences.

## 9.1    Choosing a strategy

A valuable aid to successful briefing is being able to adopt a strategy appropriate to the complexity of the building envisaged and the kind of client undertaking the project.

Upon commencement of the project, the architect will be able to give advice about the strategy to adopt. He will do this by analysing and assessing the following interrelating factors:

o     The client's experience and background.

o     The character and complexity of the project.

o     The types and mixture of the professional expertise needed to undertake the project.

o     The size of the architectural practice and how it is organized.

When choosing a strategy, it is the experience and insight of the architect which the client will be relying on. He is the one best suited to put forward the various methods and techniques to be used for the particular project to be tackled. However, the client would be well advised to make sure that a strategy is drawn up, and he should seek an opportunity to get involved in discussions about it.

The strategy offered would include the precise working methods and procedures which are thought to be best suited to the particular client, architect and design team members involved, and the character and size of the project. It would include details about such things as:

o     The extent of the client's knowledge and experience about the process of building and each of the consultant's roles in it, and how to implement it.

o     The nature of the project being undertaken.

o     The precise manner in which client and design team will be set up to relate and communicate with each other.

o     The most appropriate and practical methods of gathering information, including how the brief is to be compiled and recorded, and whether the client is to undertake all or part of these tasks.

### 9.1.1  Some factors influencing the choice of a strategy

Consider the nature of the client or client organization. For example, is the client:

o     Briefing for the first time, possibly once only in a lifetime?

o     Producing buildings on a regular basis, perhaps repeating similar kinds of buildings from time to time?

o     An expert client with a great deal of experience and in-house expertise?

o     Combining with other organizations in a building which will be used jointly?

#### A first-time client

This is an individual or small organization in the private sector commissioning an architect for the first and possibly the only time. The client is likely to be working with a small private practice, on a relatively small, inexpensive and uncomplicated project.

o      To help combat his lack of expertise and experience in briefing, and a natural ignorance of the building process, the *client* should:
—   Look for guidance from the architect about every aspect of the briefing work, and which parts of this book to refer to.
—   Respond fully to all requests by the architect for information.
—   Attend promptly to queries raised by telephone or in writing, and be sure to attend meetings and visits called for the purpose of defining the brief.
—   Provide sufficient time to act in this way.
o      The *architect* should be ready to give a positive lead to:
—   Help the client formulate and express his aims and requirements in the form of an initial brief.
—   Elicit from the client further details about his requirements at meetings or by questionnaire.
—   Record decisions and information as they come to hand.
—   Possibly, if the fee to be paid permits, compile a final brief for agreement by the client.

### A regular or repeat client

This is an individual, or an organization, with the need to commission more than one project, such as housing associations, department stores or national hoteliers; also local authority departments and other public clients with a continuous responsibility for providing a range of similar buildings.
o      If the client's own working methods and relationship with an architect on a previous project proved to be successful and harmonious:
—   Set up previous working methods and lines of communication.
—   Discuss with the architect whether improvements are needed to the previously used methods.
—   Check whether newly appointed inexperienced people are to represent the client's organization. If so, proceed as though a first-time client is involved (see above).
o      If the new project involves a similar type of building:
—   Hold a postmortem examination of the way in which a previously designed building is used and how it performs.
—   Question a large cross-section of the people presently occupying the building.
—   Monitor and evaluate how well the building has served their needs.
—   Appraise existing space use and energy costs.
—   Recall briefing information accumulated from the previous project for possible re-use, modification and adaptation.
—   Reappraise the previous brief and determine whether it still applies to the way in which the previous building now operates.

— Set up a special meeting between the client and the design team members to thrash out the implications of the results obtained from the above steps on the new brief.

o    If the client's previous experience of briefing was not satisfactory, proceed as though for a first-time client (see above). Begin with an initial brief as though beginning a completely new project.

### An expert or very experienced client

This is a large private or public organization with a staff of highly experienced personnel working to clearly defined procedures in a rolling programme of development projects, including large, technologically complex or prestigious buildings.

o    In this case the client's own methods, working procedures and documentation techniques will be well developed through frequent use. An expert client's method of briefing will most likely stem from:

— Seeing the briefing process as part of a total strategy for the organization as a whole.

— Employing an in-house advisory professional staff of architects, engineers and quantity surveyors to appraise designs and conduct prebriefing feasibility and design exercises, such as cost-in-use studies, energy conservation studies and site development studies.

— Having already chosen a site and obtained outline planning approval.

— Predetermining the amount of finance available.

— Building type design guidance notes.

— A standardized reference brief which has been developed for the particular building type, or possibly a specially formulated statement of requirements, including environmental and technical details.

o    Because so much preliminary work will have been done before an architect is commissioned, it is natural for the architect when appointed to challenge and reappraise many of the decisions already made by the client organization. He could very well:

— Respond rapidly to the total picture offered to show what can be achieved in built form to stimulate further work on the unique brief.

— Take time to assimilate all the documentation handed over, especially if a standard brief is included.

— Illustrate any serious problems inherent in the site from his viewpoint.

— Advise if the information already decided on is unnecessarily rigid and restrictive in design terms.

— Highlight any mismatch between the standardized documentation and the requirements of the unique project.
— Build mock-ups to test arrangements of special areas.
— Organize joint visits to buildings.
— Organize a two to three day long briefing conference attended
by all the client briefing team and design team members to
resolve the requirements of the unique project.
— Request that a unique brief be compiled by the client and assist
as necessary.

## *A multi-headed client*

This consists of more than one individual or organization or public
authority collaborating when commissioning a project which includes
accommodation which is to be shared or used jointly.
o      The organizational problem here is one of combining the aims
and requirements of a number of client organizations on one site or
within one built form. It demands a special and disciplined approach
by all concerned. Factors involved are:
— One organization must adopt the role of executive client and
work directly with the architect and design team.
— The other contributing organizations must act as secondary
participants and pass their requirements to the executive client.
— Each participant's full commitment to the joint project must be
obtained as early as possible in the briefing stage, to ensure that
it is not jeopardized by the late withdrawal of one party. This is
best done by completing and signing a preliminary agreement.
— The clients need to set up a joint management group to coordinate their requirements, resolve any problems which arise when
briefing is in progress and produce a homogeneous brief.
— When each client's requirements have been satisfactorily
included in a design solution, ascertain the amount of floor area
used exclusively by each client and also any shared floor areas.
This will be done by measuring from marked-up copies of the
floor plans. The result will form the basis of the joint use agreement which needs to be drawn up.
— Whilst the brief is being developed and designing is in progress,
the joint management group needs to consider the extent and
manner of their occupation of the building. This demands deciding on possible timetables for use and responsibilities for maintenance, caretaking, running of services and the proportionate
sharing of all running costs. If full agreement can be reached at
this stage, a great many problems and misunderstandings can be
avoided when the building is brought into use.

— Ensure that all design suggestions and options are seen and appraised by each of the client organizations as they are evolved.

o     The briefing and design work will need to be conducted in a manner appropriate to the skill and experience of each client organization:

— Identify the key individuals acting as liaison officer or client representative.

— Arrange for each individual to explain his own or his organization's preferred methods of working directly to the architect and executive client.

— Define the objectives of each client, including the required date of occupation.

— Look for points of conflict where an individual client's requirements overlap or impinge on the requirements of the other clients. Search for methods of resolving any points of conflict as soon as they are discovered.

### 9.1.2    Other factors influencing the choice of a strategy

The nature of the project will also have an influence, which must be weighed together with the client's experience and background. For example, the project might be:

o     A special building of exceptionally high quality with nothing written about it.

o     The adaptation or refitting of the shell of an existing building.

o     A large building having a standardized and fully documented brief, including all kinds of fine detail about preferred layouts, fittings and finishes.

o     A joint-use building involving more than one client, combining the functions of each client's existing well-documented project brief.

o     Phased work on a large project.

Each type of project will need to be tackled differently.

*A special or very high quality building with nothing written about it*
This is an unusual building which would not be built very often, requiring a great deal of research by both client and architect. Generally it will be large, prestigious and expensive, with specialized and exacting standards. It will most likely involve development of land which is regarded in the locality as extremely sensitive, attracting close scrutiny by the planning authority.

All kinds of sophisticated and special demands on a building can be researched and recorded in a brief using the methods described in this book. When the project is unusual, there is little likelihood of finding documents which will assist with the generation of a brief. Guidance notes, or even some briefing notes of a similar type of building, would be hard to find. Under these circumstances:

o      Anticipate a lengthy briefing period and provide enough time and money to support it.

o      Commission operational research specialists to undertake user surveys and identify user preferences and opinions.

o      Be prepared to commission a large project design team of professional consultants made up of an architect, environmental engineers, a building economist, quantity surveyors, additional design professions such as a landscape architect, an interior and an industrial designer, and possibly a graphic designer and other artists.

o      Form an advisory panel of technical or subject advisers, including a full complement of the client's own in-house expert staff to work with the design team.

o      Hold a briefing conference to enable all concerned to come to grips with the fundamental problems quickly.

o      Expect to compile the brief in increments.

o      Avoid closing down options until sufficiently convinced by feasibility studies and appraisals of the most appropriate design to adopt.

o      Complete the final brief only when all initial design studies are finished and an acceptable scheme design is seen to be forthcoming.

### Adaptation or refitting of an existing building

This affects the interior spaces and services within the shell of a building and the limitations of the supporting structure. This is a stage which most buildings go through during their lifetime, sometimes more than once.

The briefing operation is basically similar to briefing for a completely new building. Begin by compiling an initial brief as though it is a new project. If the brief produced when the building was originally designed is still available, it may form a useful basis for comparing the original requirements with the changed circumstances and requirements of the initial brief.

Before collecting detailed items for the brief, establish whether the building interior can be satisfactorily reshaped or reorganized:

o      Obtain a professional appraisal of the future life-expectancy of the building, taking into account current and projected legislation affecting the structure.

o      Check that the building or its site are not adversely affected by any projected development in the vicinity.

o      Monitor and evaluate how well the building is now serving users' needs, probably by means of a user survey.

o     Study all requests for improvements and consider their inclusion in the new brief.

o     Identify how individual spaces are now used and compare with the proposed uses stated in the original brief.

o     Note any mismatch between available space and present activities.

o     Ascertain costs of upkeep – items such as cleaning, maintenance and fuel, if records are available – and look for possible cost savings.

o     Check if it will be possible to continue using the building whilst reconstruction work takes place. If so, work out the means of doing so. If satisfied that the project is feasible, develop the brief as though for a new building, and progress from there.

### A large, standardized, fully documented project containing a great deal of detailed information

This is usually required by well-established and highly experienced client organizations needing a series of buildings with almost identical requirements, such as schools, old-persons' homes or hostels, hotels or army barracks.

The organizational approach in these circumstances is mainly to do with coping with the mass of information made available. The people involved must:

o     Take time to absorb the existing documentation.

o     Search for factors which are influenced by the locality and environmental characteristics.

o     Interpret the standard brief in terms of a unique brief applicable to the immediate project in hand.

o     Organize study visits to other buildings produced for the client and appraise their performance. Note all factors which need review and revision in the standard brief.

o     Obtain the reaction of users of other buildings produced by the client in carefully set up postmortem-type examinations.

### A joint-use building for more than one client

This is any project where more than one client organization collaborates in the financing and production of a building which will be used and managed jointly.

Factors concerning the collaboration of clients in the design of joint-use projects are set out on pp. 179 and 180. A procedural approach could include:

o     Forming a steering group which represents all aspects of the participating client organizations.

o     Holding a briefing conference to enable all involved to come to grips with key problems rapidly.

o     Forming client working parties to discover and resolve all specialist joint-use requirements, especially if some conflicts are apparent or likely to arise.

o     Inviting architects and designers to working party meetings.

## Phased work on parts of a large project

This applies when a projected building is divided into blocks or wings and each one is designed to be built in stages. Usually phasing is required to meet a delay in obtaining the whole of a site, or the total amount of finance required to construct the whole building.

o     Compile an initial brief to embrace the complete project.

o     Continue the briefing process for the complete building, conduct feasibility studies and prepare outline designs.

o     Develop the brief to support the design studies needed until the scheme designs are complete.

o     Divide up the project into sections which can be built separately in phases.

o     Adjust the overall scheme design if necessary to allow division into phases.

o     Adjust the scheme design of phased sections of the project to render each phase capable of operating adequately until the later phases are added.

o     Complete the brief for each of the phases to meet the projected construction starting dates.

## Phasing construction work on a large project

This applies when a projected building is to be constructed in two or three phases – first the carcass, then the interior divisions and engineering, and finally the finishes, fittings and furniture. Usually this type of phasing is required when the project timetable does not provide time for briefing and designing the complete project before beginning site works.

o     Compile an initial brief to embrace the complete project.

o     Continue the briefing process for the complete building, conduct feasibility studies and prepare outline designs.

o     Develop the brief to support the design studies until the scheme designs are complete.

o     Divide up the project into sections which are suitable for building in separate units.

o     Adjust the overall scheme design if necessary to allow division into phases.

o     Adjust the scheme design of phased sections of the project to ensure that each phase can operate adequately until the later phases are added.

o     Complete the brief in stages to suit each of the phases in good time to allow the design team to prepare the production documents and drawings to meet the projected construction starting dates, i.e.

— First stage of the brief to define the main structure or carcass.
— Second stage to determine the arrangement and environment of the interior, and settle the type and positions of partitions and doors, engineering installations and fixed equipment, and basic room layouts.
— Final brief, including all aspects of the interior design, such as finishes, fixtures, fittings, furniture, colours, textures and moveable equipment.

## 9.2    Some common techniques in general use

In addition to employing an effective strategy, various other supporting methods of working are available for briefing. Here again, the client and consultants must decide together which are appropriate to the project in hand and the particular people producing the brief and project designs.

Of the many established techniques which can be employed, the simplest involve the use of checklists and questionnaires.

There are also well-established techniques such as cost planning, or the use of briefing conferences or computer aids, which are very helpful, but may be thought too complex for all types of projects.

However, should briefing work begin and the first design exercises take place without them, the client could risk losing the opportunity of stating and clarifying all his needs and also maintaining control of the way in which the project develops.

It is wise to support the briefing work by adopting techniques which are appropriate to the project in hand. The client and architect should not be offhand about this, allowing one technique or another to be introduced in an *ad hoc* manner. They should mutually agree which techniques are to be used; then the client can be advised about his role in their operation, if this should be necessary.

Techniques which might be considered are as follows.

### 9.2.1  Checklists

Most people are used to having checklists supplied as a guide for their work. They are very much part of life, but because they are usually regarded with suspicion there is a tendency to shy away from any thought of using them. To avoid their usefulness being frustrated is a matter of knowing how best to use them.

Simply consider each item in the list as a prompt. Tick off items which are obviously irrelevant and those you already have in hand. As you work through the list, look for items you find new or interesting to work on. Periodically refer again to the checklist until all items are marked as acted upon.

## 9.2.2  Questionnaires

After receiving the client's brief, most architects and consultants will compile lists of questions which are sent to the client from time to time. Use of this simple method avoids overlooking all kinds of topics and particular pieces of information.

When responding, the client is expected to answer all questions immediately. Invariably there will be one or two items which cannot be answered properly without doing more research. But the questionnaire should not be retained on that account. Return it to the architect immediately and highlight the questions which will need more time spent on answering them.

Never give insufficiently considered answers in order to return the questionnaire promptly. If the question is not straightforward to answer, keep it as a topic for discussion with the architect at a future meeting.

## 9.2.3  Cost planning

Cost planning is a well-developed and proved method of tailoring the amount and quality of a building to meet the sum of money the client wishes to spend. By using this technique, the quantity surveyor is able to generate an initial assessment of cost from the outline brief and first design sketches. Then, as the brief develops and designs are firmed up, regular monitoring of the way in which they affect the project cost can be carried out.

If the project cost is to be successfully controlled, a number of factors need to be considered. These are as follows:

o  Check that all elements which contribute to the total project cost are included in the cost plan and are clearly defined:

—  Size and quality of the structure.
—  All parts of the building, its finishes and equipment.
—  Consultants' fees and expenses.
—  Insurances, legal fees.

o  Recognize that early projections of probable cost will be extremely rough, because they can only be based on the broad assumptions and limited information which exist at the beginning of the project.

o  Recognize that a realistic value cannot be calculated for the project until the brief and scheme design have progressed to a firm state, when decisions have been made about all quality standards and the extent and kind of the engineering installations.

o      Remember that a cost plan contains two main variable elements which if misjudged can lead to a wide variation between the estimate and the actual contract cost – sometimes called price and design reserve. These are:

—    The assessment made to evaluate price trends and the climate of tendering to be expected in the locality, shown as a percentage increase or decrease on national averages held by the industry.

—    The assessment made to accommodate tolerances which can be expected between the cost plan prices and the actual costs of elements when design drawings are ready for construction of the project.

The client should expect to receive copies of the cost plan when first compiled and again when updated as the design takes shape. Mostly the client will need some explanation of the cost statements.

To ensure that cost planning procedures are applied correctly, the client will need to rely on the professional expertise of the architect and quantity surveyor. Cost planning only works successfully if close communication exists between each member of the design team and the quantity surveyor. It depends on a high degree of collaboration and frequent communication.

### 9.2.4   Briefing conferences

Briefing conferences are a means of rapidly tuning in to the client's preferences and to key user requirements. They are expensive to set up, but they are a well worthwhile technique for use on large, complex projects.

After the outline brief has been prepared, the client and design teams meet together for two or more days of intensive work. They may choose the site of the project, the client's offices, or a secluded conference suite to work in.

Primarily, the time is used to obtain first-hand impressions of the main items which make up the outline brief and to look deeply into their relevance and importance. Also, the wider implications of the explanations given by the client can be examined, together with the potential direction in which the project could evolve.

At the conclusion of the conference, a considerable amount of data will have been collected by everyone present – client, architect and consultants alike. Many new lines of thought will have opened up. This in itself will not produce a brief, but it can create a number of things of value. For example, the participants should find they have:

o      An enhanced affiliation with the client's objectives.

o        A mutual and more detailed understanding of each others' problems.
o        A strong incentive to continue the work as a team.
o        A wider, less restrictive basis from which to build up the brief.

### 9.2.5  Design sessions

Design sessions are similar to briefing conferences, two or three day intensive working meetings which are arranged much later in the development of the brief. They cater for the pulling together of a number of strands of work – perhaps some user studies by a marketing agency, an in-depth site assessment by a research team, several cost-in-use studies by an economist and the architect's ongoing design studies. The design session will tend to act as a catalyst, producing the opportunity for those involved to report and air their views and recommendations, and for the problems and conflicts which arise to be talked over. Some off-the-cuff design options might be undertaken by the design team during the session, with the involvement of members of the client's organization. It is a valid method of pressing quickly forward to grasp a feasible design solution.

Quite short design sessions involving only the client and project architect can also be worthwhile, especially if the architect uses computer-generated graphic diagrams to produce possible plan arrangements. Time spent together using computer-aided design routines, however simple they are, can be very productive.

It is misleading to expect briefing conferences and design sessions to produce, practical concrete solutions ready for immediate further development. Usually the design team will need time to appraise the outcome and implications of the event. Wait for an architect's report on the outcome of the conference and seek his considered recommendations about developing the design.

### 9.2.6  Computing

Computers are rapidly reshaping the architect's workplace and modes of working. They are prominent in the office landscape and are an indispensable part of the design environment, largely replacing the drawing board and set square as the main precision tool for producing working drawings. Each member of the design team uses computers in a different way to support their primary skills and design routines.

Clients may think there is little support available from computers to help them with the first stages of producing a brief. Those with their own in-house computer systems tuned to supporting their business or organizational tasks may not immediately conceive how to apply computing to a new activity such as briefing.

It will be found, however, that any client, whether a large organization, a small partnership or a family group, can bring to the task of briefing the experience already obtained of computing and the use of computer networks. Most people will have used or had some contact with some of the programs set out in the chart given on p. 192, particularly those to do with information services, project management or costs and estimating. This experience, together with the prevalent use of word-processing and computer communication techniques, should prove to be a good basis for starting up good supporting systems for formulating the brief. The facilities they offer to any individual can be brought to bear on the work which has to be done when compiling and developing a brief.

*Word-processing as an aid when writing a brief*
People who write frequently and draft complex and lengthy texts depend on word-processing. It facilitates their drafting work and vastly improves the ability to edit and revise what has been written. Brief writers will also find it invaluable, particularly as a means of setting down and ordering their thoughts about the required building. When employing word-processing techniques to compile and work up a brief, the first simple steps to take are:
o    Check whether your computer is compatible with the hardware used by your architect, so that information can be transmitted directly to his system by data disks or network.
o    Check that the fax-modem software installed in your communications computer will transmit effectively to the architect's computer. If not, consider changing your modem system.
o    Ensure that *all* contributions to the brief are written using a word-processor.
    However, use of word-processing techniques allows much more scope for collecting information from other sources inside and outside the organization.
o    With the use of a scanner, texts and diagrams from text books, magazine articles or company documents can be captured as computer files for display on screen or printing out.
o    Methods of assembling and organizing contributions to the brief can be set up using an information structure such as the example given in Section 7.1.
o    Communication via private computer links using e-mail or local area networks can be established to send or receive computer files. In this way, texts, diagrams or drawings can be passed between the client, architect and consultants during the development of the brief, and whilst designs and specifications are being prepared.

o    The brief can be developed and expanded from its initial form to include more and more details as they come to hand.

o    Correcting and editing the brief to record decisions as they are taken becomes easier.

For many clients, use of these techniques will have become second nature. Fusing them into a unified project-oriented system which is understood by all staff contributing to the brief is the main objective for them. Those who are less experienced will need to approach the task using only as many of the benefits offered by computers as they feel comfortable with.

*Using other readily available computer techniques*

As a design tool

It is reasonable to suppose that computing is going to assist in other ways with the briefing and design of your project. You can be sure that the architect and other members of the design team will be using computers in the normal course of their work and it is worth considering whether some of these programs might also be of direct help to the client and his briefing team.

Most architects will have shaped and consolidated their computer working routines to suit their preferred working methods. Programs could be in regular use to assist with:

— Scheduling room requirements, collecting descriptions, specifications, diagrams and illustrations of fittings, and preferred products and materials room by room.
— Planning and analysing room relationships and circulation routes.
— Specification writing and management of the collection and working up of specifications.
— Searching out relevant British Standards, Building Regulations, EC Directives, etc.
— Selecting proprietary building products from information held about their characteristics and performance (including product images).
— Engineering and structural design calculations.
— Site modelling, studying the effect of alternative siting possibilities on the site.
— Interior layout design.
— Methods of appraising design solutions, including comparative costings.
— Visualizing by converting simple design sketches into three-dimensional forms which later on can then be rendered to produce quite realistic presentations.

— Building up a prototype of a projected building within a computer model to review the emerging design and identify any changes needed.
— Preparing design scheme and production drawings of all kinds.
— Planning and integrating engineering installations into the production drawings.

It is suggested that you:

o     Discover the computer routines which the architect and design team members use regularly.

o     Find out if there are any programs which the client group can use jointly with the architect to the benefit of the project.

o     Beware of getting involved in a program which the architect has only recently taken into use.

o     Check how successful the program has proved to be before becoming committed as a joint-user.

As a management tool

Present-day computing techniques contribute greatly to the management and timetabling of a project. They are now a well-assimilated feature of management. Computer programs which the architect and associated consultants are likely to employ are those which help with:

— Document management and checking drawings currently being worked on, highlighting the up-to-date version of all drawings and other documents on the system, and logging and tracking all activities concerning document distribution and usage.
— Planning and control of operational procedures.
— Support of project management procedures and reporting.
— Timetabling and network analysis.
— Estimating and updating of cost plans.
— Budget control and monitoring expenditure.
— Supporting the implementation and management of the CDM Regulations.
— Project risk analysis.

Again, it is suggested that you:

o     Discover the particular programs which the project manager and design team are using and ascertain whether they can serve the client organization also, perhaps by means of a direct communications link.

o     Take care only to become involved in proved and successful systems.

*Networking and CD-ROM based information*
The potential now exists for computers in an architect's design studio to become the key operational focus for gathering and editing relevant technical and product information, specification notes, site details, and

also the client's briefing material as it develops. In time, these techniques will undoubtably become more sophisticated and efficient and those clients who are able to link up directly by means of a computer network will find it adds to the success of the project.

If the communication link is made through a private telephone network, such as the *Intranet*, drawings and documents can be transferred in a secure, organized fashion on a company-wide scale. Less suitable is the *Internet*, which is open to the public for accessing corporate information only and is, of course, not secure.

Not all the information gathered into the architect's design studio is received exclusively through a computer network. Vast quantities of reference material are available on CD-ROM. Central agencies and organizations issue CD-ROM libraries of general information. The subject matter includes databases of professional practices, technical indexes, product selector and specifier's guides, the UK National Building Specification, British Standards and codes of practice, British Research Establishment Notes, and the Building Regulations. Some information is made available online, providing continually updated texts for downloading to disk each month.

To know that this vast collection of general information is accessible to the design team might reassure the client about the ability of the professionals working for him to find pertinent information vital to the project. Also, it might be possible to refer to parts of this collection himself, either directly or with the help of the architect.

*Virtually real presentations*

By employing sequences of three-dimensional computer images, a simulated walk through a projected building can be produced whilst it is still in the design stage – a prospect few clients would wish to miss. If your architect offers this facility, it would of course be irresistible. However, exciting as the experience can be, the client team would be well advised to steel themselves to view what might seem virtually real in a sober and critical way.

When viewing a walk-through presentation, do not lose sight of a few obvious things:

— It is imitating what the interior spaces will look like. It is entirely visual. An all round sense of experiencing the interior cannot be reproduced when sound, smell and touch are absent and when the effect of the continually changing quality of natural lighting conditions cannot be truly simulated.

— The images are much more faithful to forms and colours resulting from the designer's vision than can be portrayed by coloured pencil or rendered ink sketches.

— When viewed with imagination, it becomes an invaluable tool for assessing designs at a time when changes can be made relatively cheaply.

Of course, more sophisticated and complex computer software is being devised continually to assist with all kinds of project design and management tasks.

However, regardless of how useful and time-reducing it may seem, it would be prudent for any client organization to avoid using innovative programs and newly developed communication techniques on a live project. Only after being thoroughly investigated and tried out, should they be regarded as a prospect for serious use.

To obtain independent help when assessing the reliability and usefulness of particular computer programs, a client could consult computer user groups such as the *Construction Industry Computing Association* set up for this purpose in the UK at 1 Trust Court, Histon, Cambridge, or consult a computer specialist experienced in architectural systems.

---

**Types of computer programs which might assist the briefing and initial design of buildings**

| *Information services* | *Computer-aided design* |
|---|---|
| Word-processing | Design appraisal |
| Database management | Draughting systems |
| Scheduling | Perspective drawing |
| Property records | Building modelling |
| Expert systems | Site modelling |
| Financial modelling | Walk-through simulation |
| | |
| *Environmental analysis* | *Energy consumption* |
| Heat gains and losses | Energy requirements |
| Natural lighting | Plant and system |
| Noise levels | simulation |
| Ventilation | Energy consumption |
| | Running costs |
| | |
| *Costs and estimating* | *Project management* |
| Cost feasibility | Planning and control |
| Cost records – data about | Network analysis |
| existing buildings | Management reporting |
| Taking off quantities | |
| Cash flow | |

# Property condition survey forms

In common with other large client organizations, the Department of Architecture of Cheshire County Council devised a method for collecting data about the condition of their large stock of buildings. The method employed records the extent, composition and comparative condition of all the main elements and components of each building. Building surveyors assess the physical condition of building components and elements. Their findings are recorded on specially prepared forms with the use of category numbers shown on the scale set out below:

| Category | Definition |
| --- | --- |
| 1. *Hazardous* | Requires immediate attention as a matter of urgency. |
| 2. *Bad* | Generally in very bad condition – requiring priority attention. |
| 3. *Part bad* | In very bad condition in parts only, requiring priority work to those parts. |
| 4. *Poor* | In unsatisfactory condition, needing repair generally to prevent early deterioration of the component. |
| 5. *Part poor* | Generally adequate, but requiring minor repairs in part only. |
| 6. *Tolerable* | Generally good overall and working as intended. Not requiring attention in the short term. |
| 7. *Reasonable* | Very satisfactory overall and not likely to require attention for some years. |
| 8. *Good* | Good as new. |

The property condition survey forms used by Cheshire County Council are illustrated on pp. 194–197 as an example and are reproduced with their permission.

## EXTERIOR ELEMENTS
### RO ROOFING

| MAIN COMPONENTS | Code | Cat | % |
|---|---|---|---|
| Felt flat inc. perimeter treatment, drainage, etc. | RO 1101 | | |
| Asphalt inc. perimeter treatment, drainage, etc. | RO 1103 | | |
| Sheet lead inc. perimeter treatment, drainage | RO 1105 | | |
| Slates inc. flashings, verges, drainage, etc. | RO 1107 | | |
| Clay or conc. tiles, inc. verges, drainage, etc. | RO 1109 | | |
| Asbestos slates, inc. flashings, verges, drainage | RO 1111 | | |
| Metal sheeting inc. flashings, drainage, etc. | RO 1113 | | |
| Asbestos sheeting inc. flashings, drainage, etc. | RO 1115 | | |
| Felt pitched inc. perimeter treatment, drainage, etc. | RO 1117 | | |
| | | | 100 |

| SUBSIDIARY COMPONENTS | Code | Cat. |
|---|---|---|
| Metal flashings | RO 1119 | |
| Upstands and edge trims (flat roof) | RO 1121 | |
| Valley gutters (pitched roofs) | RO 1401 | |
| Metal rainwater gutters and fall pipes | RO 1406 | |
| PVC rainwater gutters and fall pipes | RO 1411 | |
| Asbestos rainwater gutters and fall pipes | RO 1416 | |
| Rooflights, patent glazing and roof windows | RO 1123 | |

### EW EXTERNAL WALLING

| MAIN COMPONENTS | Code | Cat. | % |
|---|---|---|---|
| Brickwork inc. parapet walls, chimneys, etc. | EW 1125 | | |
| Blockwork inc. parapet walls, chimneys, etc. | EW 1127 | | |
| Stonework inc. parapet walls, chimneys, etc. | EW 1129 | | |
| Rendered surfaces | EW 1131 | | |
| Slate/Tile hanging inc. flashings, trims, etc. | EW 1133 | | |
| Timber cladding, inc. flashings, trims, etc. | EW 1135 | | |
| Concrete frame and/or concrete cladding | EW 1001 | | |
| Timber curtain walling inc. infil panels, etc. | EW 1137 | | |
| Steel curtain walling inc. infil panels, etc. | EW 1139 | | |
| Aluminium curtain walling inc. infil panels, etc. | EW 1141 | | |
| Plastic coated curtain walling inc. infil panels | EW 1143 | | |
| Timber windows inc. sub. cills and ironmongery | EW 1145 | | |
| Steel windows inc. sub. cills and ironmongery | EW 1147 | | |
| Aluminium windows inc. sub. cills and ironmongery | EW 1149 | | |
| P.V.C. windows inc. sub. cills and ironmongery | EW 1151 | | |
| | | | 100 |

| | | | | |
|---|---|---|---|---|
| BLOCK REF NO. | | FISC CODE | | BLOCK NO. |
| CONSTRUCTION TYPE | | ISSUING OFFICER No. | | |
| AREA | | YEAR OF CONST. | | |
| DIVISION | | YEAR OF SURVEY | | |

### EW EXTERNAL WALLING (CONT.)

| SUBSIDIARY COMPONENTS | Code | Cat. |
|---|---|---|
| Parapet walls/copings. | EW 1153 | |
| Chimneys | EW 1155 | |
| Infil panels | EW 1157 | |
| Sub cills surrounds (stone, slate, asbestos, tiled) | EW 1159 | |
| Ironmongery (window fastenings, hinges, etc.) | EW 1161 | |
| Draught proofing (integral/applied) | EW 7101 | |
| Bedding and pointing to glazing | EW 1163 | |
| Fire Escapes inc. balustrades | EW 1165 | |

### ED EXTERNAL DOORS

| MAIN COMPONENTS | Code | Cat. | % |
|---|---|---|---|
| Softwood inc. frames and ironmongery | ED 1167 | | |
| Hardwood inc. frames and ironmongery | ED 1169 | | |
| Steel inc. frames and ironmongery | ED 1171 | | |
| Aluminium inc. frames and ironmongery | ED 1173 | | |
| Roller Shutters inc. frames and ironmongery | ED 1175 | | |
| Sliding folding inc. frames and ironmongery | ED 1177 | | |
| | | | 100 |

| SUBSIDIARY COMPONENTS | Code | Cat. |
|---|---|---|
| Ironmongery | ED 1179 | |
| Draught proofing (integral/applied) | ED 7111 | |

### EP EXTERNAL DECORATION

| | Code | | % |
|---|---|---|---|
| Overall decoration | EP 1301 | | 100 |

| SUBSIDIARY COMPONENTS | Code | Cat. |
|---|---|---|
| Timber windows and doors — painted | EP 1305 | |
| Timber windows and doors — varnished | EP 1309 | |
| Timber windows and doors — treated preservative | EP 1313 | |
| Steel windows and doors — painted | EP 1317 | |
| Wall surfaces — painted | EP 1321 | |
| Timber generally — painted | EP 1325 | |
| Timber generally — treated preservative | EP 1329 | |

## INTERIOR ELEMENTS
### CE CEILINGS

| MAIN COMPONENTS | Code | Cat. | % |
|---|---|---|---|
| Plastered surfaces | CE 1201 | | |
| Boarding or accoustic tiling | CE 1204 | | |
| Proprietary Suspended ceilings | CE 1207 | | |
| Exposed woodwool slabs/stramit | CE 1210 | | |
| Exposed metal decking | CE 1213 | | |
| | | | 100 |

| SUBSIDIARY COMPONENTS | Code | Cat. |
|---|---|---|
| Rooflight linings | CE 1216 | |
| Exposed structural members | CE 1219 | |

### FL FLOORING

| MAIN COMPONENTS | Code | Cat. | % |
|---|---|---|---|
| Wood Block inc. skirtings, etc. | FL 1222 | | |
| Granwood inc. skirtings, etc. | FL 1225 | | |
| T & G Strip Boarding inc. skirtings, etc. | FL 1228 | | |
| Concrete/grano/stone inc. skirtings, etc. | FL 1231 | | |
| Ceramic/Quarry Tiles inc. skirtings, etc. | FL 1234 | | |
| Terrazzo Tiles inc. skirtings, etc. | FL 1237 | | |
| Lino/P.V.C. sheet inc. skirtings, etc. | FL 1240 | | |
| Lino/P.V.C. tiles inc. skirtings, etc. | FL 1243 | | |
| Carpet inc. skirtings, etc. | FL 1246 | | |
| Pitch Mastic Screeding inc. skirtings, etc. | FL 1249 | | |
| | | | 100 |

| SUBSIDIARY COMPONENTS | Code | Cat. |
|---|---|---|
| Skirtings | FL 1252 | |
| Matwells | FL 1255 | |
| Floor channels and gratings | FL 1258 | |

### IW INTERNAL WALLS

| MAIN COMPONENTS | Code | Cat. | % |
|---|---|---|---|
| Exposed Brickwork | IW 1261 | | |
| Exposed Blockwork | IW 1264 | | |
| Plastered surface | IW 1267 | | |
| Plasterboard dry lining | IW 1270 | | |
| Wall tiling/glazed brickwork | IW 1273 | | |
| Specialist or glazed partitioning | IW 1276 | | |
| | | | 100 |

| SUBSIDIARY COMPONENTS | Code | Cat. |
|---|---|---|
| Balustrades and Handrails | IW 1279 | |

### ID INTERNAL DOORS

| MAIN COMPONENTS | Code | Cat. | % |
|---|---|---|---|
| Softwood, inc. linings, etc. and ironmongery | ID 1282 | | |
| Hardwood inc. linings, etc. and ironmongery | ID 1285 | | |

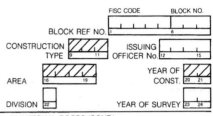

| | FISC CODE | BLOCK NO. |
|---|---|---|
| BLOCK REF NO. | 1 | 6 |
| CONSTRUCTION TYPE | 9   11 | ISSUING OFFICER No. 12   15 |
| AREA | 16   19 | YEAR OF CONST. 20   21 |
| DIVISION 22 | | YEAR OF SURVEY 23   24 |

### ID INTERNAL DOORS (CONT.)

| | Code | Cat. |
|---|---|---|
| Roller/shutter inc. track and ironmongery | ID 1288 | |
| Sliding/folding inc. track and ironmongery | ID 1291 | |
| | | 100 |

| SUBSIDIARY COMPONENTS | Code | Cat. |
|---|---|---|
| Ironmongery inc. closers | ID 1294 | |
| Panic Bolts | ID 1297 | |

### IW INTERNAL PLUMBING

| | Code | Cat. |
|---|---|---|
| All fittings and wastes | IW 1421 | 100 |

| SUBSIDIARY COMPONENTS | Code | Cat. |
|---|---|---|
| Sanitary fittings inc. taps | IW 1426 | |
| Wastes and associated pipework | IW 1431 | |
| Overflow pipework | IW 1436 | |

### IP INTERNAL DECORATION

| | Code | Cat. |
|---|---|---|
| Overall Decoration | IP 1333 | 100 |

| SUBSIDIARY COMPONENTS | Code | Cat. |
|---|---|---|
| Ceilings — painted | IP 1337 | |
| Ceilings — papered | IP 1341 | |
| Special ceiling finishes | IP 1345 | |
| Walls — painted | IP 1349 | |
| Walls — papered | IP 1353 | |
| Special wall finishes | IP 1357 | |
| Woodwork — painted | IP 1361 | |
| Woodwork — varnished | IP 1365 | |
| Iron/steel and pipework — painted | IP 1369 | |

### FF FIXED FITTINGS

| | Code | Cat. |
|---|---|---|
| All Built-in fittings | FF 1373 | 100 |

| SUBSIDIARY COMPONENTS | Code | Cat. |
|---|---|---|
| Kitchen Fittings | FF 1377 | |
| Laboratory Fittings | FF 1381 | |
| General Fittings | FF 1385 | |

## MECHANICAL SERVICES — SH SPACE HEATING

(including heat generation)
Gas ☐ Oil ☐ Coal ☐ Elect. ☐ Other ☐

| MAIN COMPONENTS — WATER | Code | Cat. | % |
|---|---|---|---|
| Air handling/Air Conditioning Systems | SH 5101 | | |
| Fan Convectors systems | SH 5105 | | |
| Natural Convector systems | SH 5109 | | |
| Radiator systems | SH 5113 | | |
| Floor coil system | SH 5117 | | |
| Ceiling system | SH 5121 | | |
| Others | SH 5125 | | |

| MAIN COMPONENTS — ELECTRICITY | Code | Cat. | % |
|---|---|---|---|
| Under Floor/coiling system | SH 6101 | | |
| Thermal Storage system | SH 6111 | | |
| On Peak system | SH 6121 | | |

| MAIN COMPONENTS — GAS IND. HEATERS | Code | Cat. | % |
|---|---|---|---|
| Convector system | SH 5129 | | |
| Radiant system | SH 5133 | | |
| | | | 100 |

| SUBSIDIARY COMPONENTS | Code | Cat. |
|---|---|---|
| Boilers | SH 5001 | |
| Burners | SH 5006 | |
| Refrigeration Plant | SH 6131 | |
| Pumps | SH 5011 | |
| Air handling plant | SH 5016 | |
| Convectors | SH 5137 | |
| Radiators | SH 5141 | |
| Filters | SH 5021 | |
| Distribution pipework | SH 5145 | |
| Insulation | SH 5149 | |
| Valves | SH 5153 | |
| Controls | SH 5301 | |
| Oil Tanks | SH 5026 | |
| Oil Meters | SH 5311 | |

### DH DOMESTIC HOT WATER

| MAIN COMPONENTS | Code | Cat. | % |
|---|---|---|---|
| Central Hot water system incl. insulation | DH 5157 | | |
| Electric local water heaters | DH 6141 | | |
| Gas local water heaters | DH 5161 | | |
| | | | 100 |

| SUBSIDIARY COMPONENTS | Code | Cat. |
|---|---|---|
| Cylinder | DH 5031 | |
| Controls | DH 5321 | |
| Insulation | DH 5165 | |
| Water meter | DH 5331 | |

### DC DOMESTIC COLD WATER

| MAIN COMPONENTS | Code | Cat. | % |
|---|---|---|---|
| Mains Cold Water system | DC 1441 | | |

---

| FISC CODE | | BLOCK NO. | | |
|---|---|---|---|---|

BLOCK REF NO. |1 | | | | |6 | | |

CONSTRUCTION TYPE |9 | |11

ISSUING OFFICER No. |12 | | |15

AREA |16 | | |19

YEAR OF CONST. |20 | |21

DIVISION |22

YEAR OF SURVEY |23 | |24

### DC DOMESTIC COLD WATER (CONT.)

| | DC 1446 | | |
|---|---|---|---|
| Tank Cold Water inc. tanks | DC 1446 | | |
| | | | 100 |

| SUBSIDIARY COMPONENTS | Code | Cat. |
|---|---|---|
| Tank (cistern) | DC 1451 | |
| Pipework | DC 1456 | |
| Insulation | DC 1461 | |
| Water Softener | DC 1466 | |
| Hose Reels | DC 1471 | |

### EV EXTRACT VENTILATION

| MAIN COMPONENTS | Code | Cat. | % |
|---|---|---|---|
| Toilets | EV 5201 | | |
| General Areas | EV 5211 | | |
| Steam/Fume extraction | EV 5221 | | |
| Dust Extraction | EV 5231 | | |
| Natural ventilation | EV 5241 | | |
| | | | 100 |

| SUBSIDIARY COMPONENTS | Code | Cat. |
|---|---|---|
| Filters | EV 5251 | |
| Fans | EV 5261 | |
| Ductwork | EV 5271 | |
| Controls | EV 5341 | |

### GD GAS DISTRIBUTION SYSTEM

| MAIN COMPONENTS | Code | Cat. | % |
|---|---|---|---|
| Natural Gas System | GD 5169 | | |
| L.P.G. System | GD 5173 | | |
| | | | 100 |

### SW SWIMMING POOL TREATMENT PLANT

| Overall Plant | SW 5036 | 100 |
|---|---|---|

| SUBSIDIARY COMPONENTS | Code | Cat. |
|---|---|---|
| Filtration Plant | SW 5041 | |
| Pool Circulation | SW 5046 | |
| Chemical Treatment Plant Auto Manual | SW 5051 | |
| Pool Cover | SW 5056 | |

### CA COMPRESSED AIR

| Overall installation | CA 5061 | 100 |
|---|---|---|

### IN INCINERATORS

| MAIN COMPONENTS | Code | Cat. | % |
|---|---|---|---|
| Bulk incinerator system | IN 5066 | | |
| Sanitary incinerators | IN 5071 | | |
| | | | 100 |

## ELECTRICAL SERVICES

Electrical supply    underground-ugd ☐    single phase sph ☐

                overhead ohd ☐    three phase tph ☐

## EXTERNAL ELEMENTS

### EL LIGHTING

| MAIN COMPONENTS | Code | Cat. | % |
|---|---|---|---|
| Pylon fixed fittings | EL 6001 | | |
| Column fixed fittings | EL 6006 | | |
| Lowerable column fittings | EL 6011 | | |
| Bollard fittings | EL 6016 | | |
| Wall mounted fittings | EL 6021 | | |
| | | | 100 |

| SUBSIDIARY COMPONENTS | Code | Cat. |
|---|---|---|
| Fluorescent fittings | EL 6026 | |
| Discharge fittings | EL 6031 | |
| Tungsten fittings | EL 6036 | |

| OTHER MAIN COMPONENTS | Code | Cat. | % |
|---|---|---|---|
| Aerial Systems | AS 6501 | | 100 |
| Lightning Conductor Systems | LC 6506 | | 100 |
| Window Cleaning hoist installation | WH 6301 | | 100 |
| Diesel/Petrol Pump Installations | PI 6511 | | 100 |

## INTERNAL ELEMENTS refer to test information before completing

### DE ELECTRICAL DISTRIBUTION

| Complete system | DE 6041 | | 100 |
|---|---|---|---|

| SUBSIDIARY COMPONENTS | Code | Cat. |
|---|---|---|
| Main switchgear | DE 6046 | |
| Sub Main Cables | DE 6051 | |
| Section and/or Distribution Boards | DE 6056 | |

### LT LIGHTING INSTALLATION

| MAIN COMPONENTS | Code | Cat. | % |
|---|---|---|---|
| Fluorescent | LI 6061 | | |
| Discharge | LI 6066 | | |
| Tungsten | LI 6071 | | |
| | | | 100 |

### SL STAGE LIGHTING

| Overall system | SL 6076 | | 100 |
|---|---|---|---|

### EM EMERGENCY LIGHTING

| MAIN COMPONENTS | Code | Cat. | % |
|---|---|---|---|
| Central | EM 6516 | | |
| Self Contained | EM 6521 | | |
| | | | 100 |

| | FISC CODE | BLOCK NO. |
|---|---|---|

BLOCK REF NO. ☐ | | | | | | 6 |

CONSTRUCTION TYPE ⧄ 9 11    ISSUING OFFICER No. 12 | | 15

AREA ⧄ 16 19

YEAR OF CONST. ⧄ 20 21

DIVISION 22

YEAR OF SURVEY 23 24

### PE ELECTRICAL POWER

| MAIN COMPONENTS | Code | Cat. | % |
|---|---|---|---|
| General Purpose | PE 6081 | | |
| Other Specialist | PE 6086 | | |
| | | | 100 |

### CR COLD ROOM

| Overall Installation | CR 6151 | | 100 |
|---|---|---|---|

### BF BLAST FREEZE

| Overall Installation | BF 6161 | | 100 |
|---|---|---|---|

### FA FIRE ALARM SYSTEM

| MAIN COMPONENTS | Code | Cat. | % |
|---|---|---|---|
| Manual | FA 6526 | | |
| Automatic | FA 6531 | | |
| | | | 100 |

### SS SECURITY SYSTEM

| Overall system | SS 6536 | | 100 |
|---|---|---|---|

### CS CALL SYSTEM/CLASS CHANGE

| Overall system | CS 6541 | | 100 |
|---|---|---|---|

### GE GENERATORS

| Overall unit | GE 6401 | | 100 |
|---|---|---|---|

### LH LIFTS AND HOISTS

| MAIN COMPONENTS | Code | Cat. | % |
|---|---|---|---|
| Lifts & Hoists Passenger | LH 6311 | | |
| Goods | LH 6321 | | |
| Stair | LH 6331 | | |
| Other | LH 6341 | | |
| | | | 100 |

### SH SPACE HEATING

| MAIN COMPONENTS — ELECTRICITY | Code | Cat. | % |
|---|---|---|---|
| Under floor/coiling system | SH 6101 | | ⧄ |
| Thermal storage system | SH 6111 | | ⧄ |
| On-Peak system | SH 6121 | | ⧄ |

### DH DOMESTIC HOT WATER

| Electric local water heaters | DH 6141 | | ⧄ |
|---|---|---|---|

Fuses and double insulation give little or no protection from electrocution.
● ¼ amp can kill but will now blow a fuse.
● Most accidents are caused by cut or frayed cables, loose connections, exposure to humid or damp environments, contact with water, misused or faulty equipment.

Residual current circuit breakers (RCCB's) provide the only real protection against electrocution or serious injury from electrical accidents.

**PowerBreaker-S**
PowerBreaker-S senses a tiny amount of electricity flowing to earth, through a human body, for example, and cuts off the current in a split second. **It is also intelligent enough to self-test every time the OFF button is used.**

# Bibliography

## General background reading

National Joint Consultative Committee of Architects, Quantity Surveyors and Builders, *Client's Guide: the role of the client in the design of buildings*. RIBA Publications, 1973

National Economic Development Office, *Before You Build: what a client needs to know about the Construction Industry*. Her Majesty's Stationery Office, 1974

National Economic Development Office, *The Professions in the Construction Industry*. Her Majesty's Stationery Office, 1976

*Building for Industry and Commerce: client's guide*. The Chartered Institute of Building, London, 1980

CIRIA, *A Client's Guide to Traditional Contract Building*. Special Publication 29, Construction Industry Research and Information Association, London, 1984

O'Reilly, J.J.N., *Better Briefing Means Better Buildings*. Building Research Establishment Report, Department of the Environment, London, 1987

Caudill, W.W., *Architecture by Team*. Van Nostrand Reinhold, New York, 1971

Pina, W., *Problem Seeking: an architectural programming primer*. Cahners Books International, Boston, 1977

*How to Control the Quality of a Management Consulting Engagement*. Association of Consulting Management Engineers, New York, 1966

Senior, D., *Your Architect*. Hodder and Stoughton, 1964 (now out of print)

## Briefing and design guides and aids

Konya, A., *Library Buildings: a briefing and design guide*. Butterworth Architecture, London, 1986

Konya, A., *Sports Buildings: a briefing and design guide*. Butterworth Architecture, London, 1986

*Plan of Work for Design Team Operation*. Reprinted from the *RIBA Handbook*, 1973 edition, RIBA Publications, London, 1973

Green, R., *The Architect's Guide to Running a Job*. Butterworth Architecture, London, 1962

Construction Industry Council, *Project Management Skills in the Construction Industry*. RIBA Publications

Lock, D., *Project Management*. Gower, Aldershot, 1992

Royal Institute of British Architects, *Health and Safety: Guidance for Clients on Health and Safety – The Construction (Design and Management) Regulations 1994*, RIBA Publications, London, 1995

Royal Institute of British Architects, *Guidance for Clients on Fees*, RIBA Publications, London, 1994

Royal Institute of British Architects, *Engaging an Architect: Architect's Services – Small Works*, RIBA Publications, London, 1996

## Research papers

O'Reilly, J.J.N., *A Case of a Design Commission: problems highlighted; initiatives proposed*. Building Research Establishment Current Paper, London, 1973

*Brief Formulation and the Design of Buildings*. A research paper written on behalf of the Building Research Establishment by the Buildings Research Team at the Department of Architecture, Oxford Polytechnic, Oxford, 1981

*A Design/Cost Theory for Measuring Buildings*. Occasional Paper No. 1, Department of Construction Management, University of Reading, Reading, 1982

# Addresses of professional bodies

**Architects**

The Royal Institute of British Architects (RIBA)
66 Portland Place, London W1N 4AD
Tel. 0171-580 5533

The Royal Incorporation of Architects in Scotland (RIAS)
15 Rutland Square, Edinburgh EH1 2BE
Tel. 0131-229 7205

The Royal Society of Ulster Architects
2 Mount Charles, Belfast BT7 1NZ
Tel. 01232 323760

The American Institute of Architects
1735 New York Avenue, NW, Washington DC 20006-5292
Tel. 202 626 7300

**Building Surveyors**

The Royal Institute of Chartered Surveyors (RICS)
12 Great George Street, Parliament Square, London SW1P 3AD
Tel. 0171-222 7000
*and*
9 Manor Place, Edinburgh EH3 7DN
Tel. 0131-225 7078

**Engineers**

The Association of Consulting Engineers
Alliance House, 12 Caxton Street, London SW1H 0QL
Tel. 0171-222 6557

The Chartered Institute of Building Services
222 Balham High Road, London SW12 9BS
Tel. 0181-675 5211

The American Institute of Consulting Engineers
345 East 47th Street, New York, NY 10017

American Consulting Engineers Council
1015 15th Street, NW, Suite 802, Washington DC 20005
Tel. 202 347 7474

## Interior Designers
Chartered Society of Designers
32–38 Saffron Hill, London EC1N 8FH
Tel. 0171-831 9777

The American Institute of Interior Designers
730 Fifth Avenue, New York, NY 10019

American Society of Interior Designers
608 Massachusetts Avenue, NE, Washington, DC 20002
Tel. 202 546 3480

## Landscape Consultants
The Landscape Institute
6–7 Barnard Mews, London SW11 1QW
Tel. 0171-738 9166

The American Institute of Landscape Architects
501 East San Juan Avenue, Phoenix AZ 85012

American Society of Landscape Architects
4401 Connecticut Avenue, NW, 5th Floor, Washington DC 20008-2302
Tel. 202 686 2751

## Land Surveyors
The Royal Institute of Chartered Surveyors (RICS)
12 Great George Street, Parliament Square, London SW1P 3AD
Tel. 0171-222 7000
*and*
9 Manor Place, Edinburgh EH3 7DN
Tel. 0131-225 7080

## Quantity Surveyors
The Royal Institute of Chartered Surveyors (RICS)
12 Great George Street, Parliament Square, London SW1P 3AD
Tel. 0171-222 7000

*and*
9 Manor Place, Edinburgh EH3 7DN
Tel. 0131-225 7078

# Index